AS IF IT WERE

poems

AS IF IT WERE

FRED CHAPPELL

For Tim and Cynthia —

Blessings on you!

Fred Clapp.15

LOUISIANA STATE UNIVERSITY PRESS

Baton Rouge

Published by Louisiana State University Press
Copyright © 2019 by Fred Chappell
All rights reserved
Manufactured in the United States of America
FIRST PRINTING

DESIGNER: Mandy McDonald Scallan
TYPEFACE: Whitman
PRINTER AND BINDER: Sheridan Books, Inc.

"Fox and Briar" and "Shepherd and Hound": *The James
Dickey Review;* "Black Cat and Evening Star" and "Truce":
Modern Age; "Fox and Crow" and "The Cat and the Two
Sparrows": *Virginia Quarterly Review;* "The Wolf, the Fox,
and the Ape:" *Carolina Mountains Literary Festival Anthology;*
"Lion Protector of the Hares," "Of Privilege," "Pru and Fancy,"
"Despot and Jester," and "Of Experience": *North Carolina
Literary Review;* "The Willful Child": *Spectral Realms;* "Fox
and Grape" appeared as a broadside from Scuppernong
Books, 2018.

Library of Congress Cataloging-in-Publication Data
Names: Chappell, Fred, 1936– author.
Title: As if it were : poems / Fred Chappell.
Description: Baton Rouge : Louisiana State University Press,
[2019]
Identifiers: LCCN 2018034714| ISBN 978-0-8071-6960-5
(pbk. : alk. paper) | ISBN
    978-0-8071-6962-9 (pdf) | ISBN 978-0-8071-6961-2 (epub)
Classification: LCC PS3553.H298 A6 2019 | DDC 811/.54--
dc23
LC record available at https://lccn.loc.gov/2018034714

Dedicated to

Ed and Becky Anderson

with all gratitude

They say the world's a child no longer. I concur—
But must amuse it still as if it were.

—LA FONTAINE

CONTENTS

Fable 1

Social Class

Advice to the Trees 5

Saving Face 7

The Bull and the Mouse 9

Fox and Briar 11

The Ass and the Pig's Barley 12

The Mischievous Dog 13

The Peacock and the Crane 15

Peacock and Juno 16

The Jay Adorned with Peacock Feathers 19

Beauty Pageant 21

The Hunter and the Lion 23

The Bearded She-Goats 26

Fox and Leopard 27

The Lioness and the Vixen 28

Of Presumption 29

Rose and Amaranth 32

The Horse and the Ass 34

Social Function

Tact Intact 37

Fox and Crab 38

The Wolf and the Lamb 39

The Nightingale and the Swallow 41

The Old Shepherd and the Ass 44

Paper and Ink 45

The Selfie and the Selfless 46

The Cock and the Pearl 48

Confession 49

A Martyr to the Cause 50

Wolf and Crane 51

Of Innovation 52

The Cat and the Cock 54

The Cat and the Two Sparrows 56

The Lion and the Melodious Ass 58

The Serpent's Head and the Tail 61

Wolf and Shepherds 63

The Cat and the Birds 66

The Wolf, the Fox, and the Ape 67

The Lion, the Wolf, and the Fox 69

Truce 71

Doctor Wolf 72

The Soothsayers 74

The Horse and the Soldier 79

The Sickly Stag 82

The Old Man and His Grandson 83

The Lion Grown Old 85

Psychology

The Eagle, the Cat, and the Wild Sow 89

The Wolf and the Dove Gathering Twigs 93

The Two Frogs 94

The Bald Man and the Fly 95

Angel and the Knot of Vipers 97

Of Extortion 98

Fly 100

The Lion Defeated by a Man 101

Motivation 103

Shepherd and Hound 105

The Bear and the Gardener 106

An Unjust Fate 111

The Old Woman and the Wine Jar 112

The Wasp and the Snake 114

The Navigator 115

Philosophy

Pru and Fancy 119

The Farmer and the Apple Tree 121

Of Experience 122

The Fox and the Man Counting Waves 126

The Child and the Book 129

Despot and Jester 131

Of Privilege 133

Lion Protector of the Hares 134

Creature 135

Ground Level 136

Image 138

Folktale

The Man Who Buried His Treasure 141

Paddock 144

The Willful Child 146

Birds and Priest 149

The Story of Saint Felix 152

King and Pirate 156

The Three Cocks 160

Spider and Turtle 163

Of a Fisherman 166

Pique 169

The Hare Who Was Married 171

Fabulists

Moralist and Fabulist 175

The Two Bald Men 178

The Dog Giving Up His Prey 180

The Ape 182

Aesop and His Illustrator 183

Aesop to Fox 186

Vixen to Aesop 188

Aesop at the Shipyard 190

Fox

Fox and Crow 195

Fox and Turkeys 196

The Streamlined Fox 198

The Fox and the Cat 200

Fox and Corncrib 202

The Fox and the Horse 203

Fox and Bust 207

Fox and Grape 209

Parable

Parable of the Trees 215

The Parable of Nathan 217

The Wheat and the Tares 219

The Leaven 220

Go For It 221

Black Cat and Evening Star 222

The Boasting Lamp 223

The New and the Old 224

Preambles/Postambles

    Social Class 225

    Social Function 226

    Psychology 227

    Philosophy 228

    Folktale 228

    Parable 229

    Fabulists 230

    Fox 231

AS IF IT WERE

Fable

When we stroll through a provincial town in ancient Greece, Sicily, Spain, or elsewhere during periods from, say, 300 BCE to 800 CE, we encounter fable figures everywhere. Representations of the Tortoise and the Hare, the Eagle and the Sow appear on the walls of arenas, schools, taverns, and alleyways. On market day storytellers professional and amateur retell the tales they like to attribute to the legendary Aesop, adding improvisations for the pleasure of surprise. On platforms and daises actors and mimes perform the roles of Fox and Bear, Aphrodite and Zeus, Mouse and Ox. Often they wear masks; often they sing and dance. These Crows and Asses are familiar to the citizens who have known them since childhood as extensions of the family of humankind. They recognize their standings in this family and identify each of them as belonging to a flexible but definable station.

A fable is a short narrative that delineates through speech and action some parts of the organizational design of the universe in which it takes place. To that end, the narrative is almost always concerned with relationships between different parts of nature which serve as actors in the story. From gods to grasses, from animals to oceans, all natural entities, including divinities, speak and perform at the will of the fabulist, confirming the existence of a stable order. Each entity acts in accordance with its inherent character. The interactions between them take the form of often fatal comedies of manners.

There are exceptions, but by and large the fable imposes a barrier against social chaos. It is a conservative art form, with the strengths and weaknesses of that outlook.

Preamble Number One, "Social Class," is an attempt provisionally to schematize the class structure of the fables. By a majority of votes, the Poems herein have relegated the prose Preambles to the rear of this volume. The verses fear contamination by an inferior species of literary composition. Historians, novelists, and philosophers have protested this arbitrary assumption of privilege by the verses and are bringing the dispute before the Court of Literary Critics who deem themselves Supreme.

Thus the hapless Preambles have become Postambles, prefatory no longer. The cursory notes to part I, "Social Class", begin on page 225, followed by the submissive other Preambles.

1

SOCIAL CLASS

Advice to the Trees

—BABRIUS

"Our inexorable, unjust fate
We have too long undergone,"
Complained the multivocal grove
        To Jove.

"We achieve majestic height
And then are toppled one by one
By the Logger's insatiable axe
In his daily sharp attacks.
Our intricate green canopy
Shelters animals cheerfully
And offers mast and other food
To a hungry multitude,
While the Logger does not heed
Any other creature's need.
We must discover means to stop
Our being harvested as a crop."

Jove said: "You can protect yourselves
By halting Logger's supply of helves.
Hear my elementary instruction:
Do not abet your own destruction.
Lacking the handle that serves as lever,
A hunk of iron is harmless ever.
Sometimes one's felicity
Lies in a becoming modesty.
Imitate the twisted laurel,
Among the humblest of the arboreal,
And then no Turner will be able
To turn you to a billiards table;

Ivy does not contribute wood
To harm itself—and never could.
Duly aspire to lowly condition
And so avoid widespread attrition."

"Great Jove, I mean no disrespect
If such advice I must reject,"
Declared a towering Longleaf Pine.
"I'd rather die than be a Vine."

Saving Face

—BABRIUS

Up leapt the Lion. He looked all about.
"Such insolence I will not tolerate!
Whoever mussed my mane will meet a fate
        He will not love to meet."

A Fox of humorous bent stood near who said,
"Your Majesty, why bother to arouse
The Court? Your troubler was a little Mouse
        Who hastily has fled."

"My realm I rule by might, also by mane,
And if a single hair is out of place,
My royal profile I do not retain
        And lose some note of grace."

"But, Majesty, we all experience
What we have come to call our Bad Hair Days,
And finally it makes no difference
        If one lone tendril strays."

"Perhaps the circumstance that you relate
Is true of those for whom cosmetic art
Is merely fashion, but a Potentate
        Must always look the part.

"My subjects will believe what they perceive;
They never would accept a Royal Pig
Or trust a King who, aiming to deceive,
        Wore as his mane a wig.

"Go find that Mouse and make him comprehend
That he should never forage recklessly;
Authority lies largely, at the end,
    In what folks think they see.

"Order in the Barber with eager shears
And clever comb to restore the King's appearance;
People must know I tend their cares and fears
    Despite Mouse interference."

The Bull and the Mouse

—AESOP

"Why did you bite me?"
Cried the startled Bull with a furious bellow.
"A brave and honorable fellow
Would stay to fight me.
You nip and scuttle into your hole
Beneath the farmyard wall."

Like a wary scout
Mouse peered out
And looked about.

"You shall pay with your piffling life,
For I shall trample you, your wife
And children, one and all,
When I thump down this wall."

He butted the wood
As hard as he could,
Yet still it stood.

For longer than an hour
He struck with all his power
While Mouse hid safe inside his Hole,
Evading Bull
And watching without a peep
Until the exhausted Bovine fell asleep.

Then out crept Mischief Mouse
From his cozy little house
To bite the Bull again
Just beneath his chin
And make another fleet
And gigglesome retreat.

The stout Bull was astounded,
Baffled and dumbfounded,
For he had given Mouse no cause
For violent enmity.
He never had transgressed the laws
Of hospitality.
In fact, he took such little note
That of the Mouse he never thought.
But now he understood that Mouse was present—
And found the circumstance unpleasant.

Bull never found a solution
For his existential confusion,
Concluding, as mortal creatures must,
The world we live in is unjust.

MORAL.

Impudent Mice will often despise
Animals of greater size;
Sometimes the good and great
Receive but do not merit hate.

Fox and Briar

—AESOP

A Fox attempted to leap a fence
And snatch a Lamb from the pasture side.
But he misjudged and, to break his fall,
Clutched a Briar which scored his hide
    And maimed his confidence.

"You offered me no help at all
    And caused me sharpish pain."

"Yes, that is true," the Briar replied,
"But you should not complain.
I can never stand alone;
I enclasp others to survive
And have no sure support to give.
Clinging to sturdier I must do;
To cling to me emperils you.
Do not upon a dependent depend,
For he will prove an unhelpful friend."

The Ass and the Pig's Barley

—PHAEDRUS

When Farmer John slaughtered a Boar
There stood a more than ample store
Of barley gathered shortly before.

"Dole these leftovers to my Ass;
He must be tired of chewing grass
And longs for food of gourmet class."

The Ass declined to taste this food.
Sadly to Farmer John he said,
"Your barley did the Pig no good.

"I shall consume my green legume;
Its fresh aroma is sweet perfume.
Barley-eating would seal my doom."

Postscript.

Upon the Pig's memorial slate
These words of Ass are gravely writ:
Perhaps the cause was something he ate.

MORAL.
In the matter of nutrition
Best keep your proper social station.

The Mischievous Dog

—AESOP

Fice Dog

"All day long you're on my case,"
Said the yappety little Fice
To the stalwart guardian of the house,
A German Shepherd named Big Claus.
"You tell me I must mend my ways,
You claim I make a pointless noise,
Exhibiting sore lack of poise.
I am, you say, a noxious pest,
A brash annoyance to every guest.
'Shut up!' you say. 'Give it a rest!
As pup-dogs go, you're a total waste!'

"But gaze upon this shiny medal
Master appended to my collar;
Its proud inscription is bound to settle
Which of us now stands the taller
In his esteem. Big Claus is old,
Too feeble a guard of our household."

Big Claus

"You bite the man who brings the mail;
You nip Pussycat on her tail,
Seeming always to forget
She is our Mistress's favorite pet.
And then, what shows you most a scoundrel,
You mauled our lady's satin sandal."

Thus Big Claus admonished the pup:
"My advice is, Give it up!
Settle down and search to find
Ways to cultivate your mind.
You may possibly have a need
Very quickly to learn to read.
Those words upon the medal you sport
Give all comers a timely report:"

little manic
BAD DOG

The Peacock and the Crane

—AESOP

"Have you admired my sumptuous finery?"
Inquired the Peacock of the Sandhill Crane.
"It adds the sheen of gold embroidery
To brilliant hues of blue and emerald green.
I strut the runway between the barn and shed,
An awe-inspiring rainbow on parade.
Your plumes are a puddle-muddle of gray and brown.
Your dull appearance wears a permanent frown.
I must disclose that I feel sorry for you."

"I reject condolence from a parvenu.
True, my plumage might seem rather shoddy
To untutored viewers who adore the gaudy.
But does not so much glitter weigh you down?
No one reports that you have ever flown.
Surf fishing is my daily occupation,
As well as my inherited vocation.
When sport no longer charms I sail the sky
Or march the gleaming beaches jauntily.
I explore my soul when I explore the azure
Heaven, while you stand stuck in cow manure.
I do not share your taste for stinking muck,"
Said Crane to the prismatical Peacock.

Peacock and Juno

—LA FONTAINE, II, 17

Peacock petitions Management:

"Great Juno, Queen
Of Air and Darkness, hear my complaint.
Last night I heard
A Mockingbird
Serenade the serene,
Complaisant Moon.

"He caused my heart to weep
With his languorous sweep
Of melting arpeggio,
His melancholy sanglot,
His nimble octave leap,
His staccato chirp and peep,
And legato note so like a moan
I borrowed it for my own.

"He sang so thrillingly I quite forgot
His insignificant physique:
A touch of black upon a smear of gray,
Barely visible as he skims away,
In flight at morning a mere dot
Against the splendor of daybreak.

"By your generosity, O Queen,
Peacock is seen
As the most splendidly attired
Of any bird.
In any beauty competition
I seize the prize,
A marvel to admiring eyes.

But in the musical category
          I earn no glory,
No crown of bays, no clutch of roses.
The judges stop their ears and hold their noses.
          I will not shame myself to repeat
Their commentary. It is not sweet.

"Do you not think it only fair
 My vocal ability should square
With my visual magnificence?
To delight but a single sense
Disappoints an audience
Long accustomed to expect
Gratification in every respect."

"Of all the ingrates I have known
You stand out as Number One;
Blue Jays may fuss, Sparrows complain,
But you are the champion Royal Pain,"
          The goddess replies.

"You adulate your splendid appearance.
I conferred on you the very essence
Of the glamour of iridescence,
Instilled in you a mettlesome spirit
Fit for one who draws my chariot
          Across the skies.
Now you grouse and gripe and bitch
Because you long for perfect pitch;
Dissatisfied with your regal tail,
You wish to sing like the Nightingale.
Do you believe great Hercules
Envies Aphrodite's knees
          And mopes and sighs?

"Upon this moment I decree
You shall be tail-less annually
And shed your grandiose panoply
Into the smelly barnyard debris
        A-swarm with flies.
It shall in season be restored
If I am devotedly adored
And if you change your attitude
To something resembling gratitude.
        Otherwise,
Your gay and beautiful display
I may completely snatch away,
Revealing for the world to see
How comical is vanity."

MORAL.
If you strut and flaunt your tail,
Disaster follows without fail.

The Jay Adorned with Peacock Feathers

—LA FONTAINE, IV, 9

When Peacock tires of plumage he wore this year
   He strips it off and lets it lie
      Wherever,
      Anywhere,
While he awaits the advent of the new.
We uppity Human Beings are not so clever,
Unsheathing credit cards to shop and buy,
     Replenishing our diminished supply.

   Peacock feathers in the dirt
   Caught the attention of an alert
    And homely upstart Jay
Who pieced the plumes together for the display
     He called his Rainbow Suit.
   Through the barnyard he would strut
Like a buff male model on his flash runway,
Not realizing that the Cock and Hens,
    The Pigs and Piglets in their pens,
    The Calf called Molly, the grinning Collie,
Even the Weathervane atop the barn
     Viewed him with condescending scorn.

Against the jokes they made at his expense
    The Jay could mount no apt defense;
     He fluttered off and meekly hid
    His embarrassment in the milking shed,
    Understanding much too late
    Peacock's finery could never fit.

La Fontaine composed this little story,
                    His angry allegory
            Against that noxious race of pests,
                    The Plagiarists.
            He could not know that I
    In a later greedy century
                    Would read with envious eyes—
                    And plagiarize.

    But I will not apologize:
    No qualms made the Frenchman stop
    Purloining it from great Aesop,
One of his most pointed fabliaux . . .
Wherefrom Aesop stole it, God only knows.

Beauty Pageant

—SUSAN NICHOLLS CHAPPELL

Within the poultry yard
Behind the house with double gable
Where Merrick Avenue crossed Bernard
In a snug suburban neighborhood
Stood two poplars and a maple,
Fenced in with whitewashed club-oak wood.
This property they shared
With an array of Ornamental Bird.

A Golden Cockerel was present,
The Cockatoo, the Cockatiel,
The Golden Pheasant
With legendary tail.
Ancient Peruvian stock
Furnished the flock with a Cock-of-the-Rock;
And the most amazing bird to view,
A white Peacock, marched to and fro.

A Cochin China with featherduster legs,
A Midnight Duck that laid black eggs,
A pink Minorca and a Burrowing Owl,
A swift Kingfisher with royal scowl,
A Magpie in a cheap tuxedo,
A supercilious albino Crow:
These and another twenty-three
Completed the avian menagerie.

A passing plump Rhode Island Red
From a Farmer's truck surveyed
This fashion-conscious clique and said,
"Have you no purpose but to adorn?

We farmyard fowl hold you in scorn
For your tiresome preening, and what is more—
What the hell are you good for?"

An elegant, clever, curvebill Merganser
Took upon herself to answer:
"Our mission? To add the touch of grace
To our every ambient space.
We are Birds allotted the duty
Of supplying desirable beauty
To the environs as we are able.
Appearance is our utility,
Our natal responsibility,
And it may someday come to pass
That at demand of an ardent foodist,
In the apparel of a nudist,
You will *decorate* a table."

The Hunter and the Lion

—AESOP

Such a personage as this Hare
The Lion never had met before.
Jangling from head to toe with gear,
Weaponed as if going to war,
With a blunderbuss and a scimitar,
With camouflage concealing each ear,
And a cotton medal brightening his rear,
The Hare presented a sight so rare
That mating Squirrels left off to stare.

The Lion in a tone polite
Asked what task he was about.

"Please speak softly," the Hare implored.
I seek the animal that is lord
Of every other animal,
Whether it be big or small,
Whether it forages its food
From dusty plain or shadowy wood.
I seek the Lion great of heart,
Mightiest of beasts, by all report.
But let us moderate our voices,
Lest we alarm him with suspicious noises."

"Perhaps I know this King you seek
Pray tell me, what does Lion look like?"

"I must admit, with sharp regret,
I have not seen a Lion as yet,
But the Tiger, Leopard, and Jaguar
Cringe and tremble at his roar;

Every predator obeys the law
That he has written with his claw.
Needing no scepter, no gilded throne,
The Lion stands as Monarch alone."

"You tell only what is known
To all us animals under the sun,
But you omit the principal thing:
Why are you anxious to meet this King?"

"If I once discover his track,
I will mount a fierce attack
And add a very special glory
To my sportsman history.
Let me first detect his spoor
Then I will trace him to his lair.
While he lounges in his den,
I'll draw my sword and do him in."

"I never thought the Hare by nature
To be a fearsome, bloodthirsty creature.
Why does Lion so inspire
In your heart such angry fire?"

"Speaking as individual,
I can live, causing no fear,
With almost any animal.
I only want the world aware:
Here lies Lion, slain by Hare."

"But Lions are scare and Hares a-plenty;
Only this morning I counted twenty.

Present-day Royalty is in decline,
Including particularly the Lion.
The marksman whom the Humans bless
Is one who widows a Lioness.
The most ordinary fate to befall
A Lion? —His head upon a study wall.
Tell me, that I may comprehend,
Why give his life a premature end?"

"So all will know I am strong and brave
And post *Lion-Slayer* at my grave
For every passerby to see."

"To slay a Lion, try killing me."

He bared his teeth with a languorous yawn;
Upon that instant Hare was gone,
Shedding in his haste to flee
His total untested armory,
As speedy in his quaint departure
As an arrow loosed by a Scythian archer.

MORAL.
Do yourself a healthy favor;
Never rattle a puny saber.

The Bearded She-Goats

—PHAEDRUS

To the Society of Masculine Goats
            Great Jove replied:
"Because the Females of your race objected
        That, while they owned identical coats
        And equally useful horns and hide,
I formed them beardless, a fault they wished corrected.
        I gave their petition gravest thought,
                While their incessant bleat
                Disturbed my judicious mind,
                And decided that the *She's*
        Should bear chin-tufts as do the *He's*.
Goatees will now be common to all your kind,
        And all your kind will live in peace.

                "But now you come to say
                That you foresee a day
                Females will wrest command
        Because they sport the emblem of
        The power that sets some Goats above
                The beardless in their band.
        But if we were to enumerate
        Those citizens of Nature's state
                That wear a beard—
The bearded mussel, iris, oat and wheat,
        The parish priest, the scarlet oak—
We name those whom the Goat has never feared.
            If you anticipate
        From bearded ladies your defeat,
You are the butts of a revealing joke."

Fox and Leopard

—AESOP

"Am I not the loveliest creature?"
The Leopard of the Fox inquired.
"Observe my features formed by Nature:
    Always splendidly attired
In a golden coat arrayed with spots,
    Lots and lots of beauty spots,
My tail as supple as the swallow's flight,
Eyes that gleam in the deep midnight,
Seductive whiskers, burnished claws
That fitly adorn my graceful paws—
    And did I mention beauty spots,
    Lots and lots of beauty spots?"

"To the claims you make I will assent,
But mine is the Stoic temperament.
Your masterpiece of cosmetic art
Does not palpitate my heart;
I do not think I shall grow wise
By seeing spots before my eyes.
My Ideal is of superior kind:
A tranquil Soul and spotless Mind.
Outward appearance merely mocks."

"So says every ugly Fox."

The Lioness and the Vixen

Of what shall Foxes proudly boast?
—Well, if the Vixen is a mother,
She will declaim like many another
Upon her genius offspring, most
Intelligent from coast to coast,
And never the leastest cause for bother.

One Vixen mentioned to a Lioness
In casual course of neighborly chat,
Matrons gossiping of this and that,
How her litter numbered four,
While her friend birthed one—with no encore.

"Your count is accurate, I will confess,
But, as my bearded husband says,
I bring a Lion into existence
While you produce another instance
Of a common, insignificant breed
For which the world has little need."

Her cruel remark did not result
In the intended harsh insult.
One of the reliable paradoxes
Is, that in a mother's sight,
Every one of her Kits by right
Stands a Lion among the Foxes.

Of Presumption

—GESTA ROMANORUM, LXXIX

Her Highness the Queen was tres petite
    And loved to play the flute;
Her stature was about five feet,
    Give or take a foot.
She practiced with her instrument,
    Tweet tweet toot tweet toot toot.

She owned a noisy little Dog
Not much larger than a Frog
    Whose name was Small Mishap.
He watched her most adoringly
    While sitting in her lap
And singing out most merrily
    Yip-yap, yap-yip, yap-yap.

But gruff King Broadbeard lacked all passion
    For Fice Dogs and for Terriers,
Regarding them as fads of fashion
    For Girls and foppish Courtiers.
His choice of pet was a gloomy Bear
    Whose gnawing jealousy
Of loud, diminutive Small Mishap
    Was obvious to see.

"Why should that puerile character
    Enjoy the Queen's affection
While with a gallant, handsome Bear
    She disdains all connection?"

So Bruin thought, and further thought
    To change the situation,
Persuading the Queen to improve his lot
    Through warm ingratiation.
"She likes a chap to sit her lap,"
    So reasoned the rotund Bear.
"That is the place to plead my case,
    So I shall lodge me there
And growl no more. My voice will soar
    Into a register
So high and sweet that from my seat
    I'll harmonize with her."

And so Bear bore six hundredweight
    Of fat and bristly fur
To the gilded throne Her Highness sat
    And plumped it all on her
And sounded a note so like the howl
    Of chipmunks baying the moon
That Broadbeard thought he'd swallowed whole
    An out-of-tune bassoon.

The Queen said nothing. How could she?
    She could not pray or swear
Or enunciate grand oratory
    From underneath the Bear.

He pressed on her like a ton of butter,
    Then heard a muffled yap
Such as Queens can never utter
    Without a Small Mishap.

"Bruin!" cried Broadbeard from his throne,
      "You commit a dark disgrace
By seating yourself upon my Queen
      And irritating Fice.
What obsessive, mad furor
      Has seized upon your mind?
She tolerated you before—
      But never your behind."

Obedient to the Royal Scowl,
      Bruin stood and bowed
And may have growled a surly growl—
      But certainly not out loud.
His venture brought his brief renown
      Tumbling down in ruin;
Ever his name will proclaim his shame:
      Queen-Flattener Bruin.

MORAL.
To limit your file of catastrophes,
Research your true capacities.

Rose and Amaranth

—AESOP

Rose

I am beautiful, you say,
   A joy to the amative eye,
      The flower that day on day
         All cherish and glorify
      With art, romance, and song
   Through many a century,
Compelling me to belong
To a reverend history.

My span is brightly brief,
   A pink or scarlet spot
      That is and then is not;
         The blossom and the leaf
         Display a fleeting life
      Before embracing earth
   That lately gave them birth
And unperceivable grief.

         Brevity, you may suppose,
         Is the sorrow of the Rose.

Amaranth

Rose, you actually lived,
   Were not vain fantasy
      Conceived by poetry
         No one ever believed
         Without being deceived.
      A different being I,
      For Immortality
   The symbol poets chose—
And not the fragile Rose.

32

You have obeyed the sun,
  You have inhaled the rain,
    And when the sun sank down
    Befriended the lonely moon.
  I never shall exist
  But as a picture of
The longing to persist,
To flourish and to love.

      Bodiless, I am weary
      Of being imaginary.

MORAL.

*Shall mortal grievers weep and sigh
If Immortality might wish to die?*

Amarontos [Greek]: "unfading." Symbol of immortality employed by classical poets, Spenser, Milton, and others of note.

The Horse and the Ass

The Ass bemoaned his unjust load
Of bricks and stones, nail kegs and wood:
"These cruel weights will do me in," he said.
 "Friend Stallion, might you lend your aid?
You're handsom, strong, and much the better fed."

"Silence, Peasant! In me you see a Steed,
 A figure Fortune has decreed
Shall never plow the sod or draw a sled.
I have discovered in my time no need
 To be concerned with daily food.
 As long as I retain my speed
 My Groom maintains a generous mood."

The Ass replied by toppling over dead.

The Groom decided now the beast should ride
 On horseback all the farther way.
 He skinned the Ass, bound on the hide,
 Not caring that the Horse pled *Nay*.

MORAL.
No matter what we claim to be,
We share a common equality;
Every member of the Upper Class
Sooner or later will bear his Ass.

Social Function

Tact Intact

—BABRIUS

A Crab suggested that he mediate
When Whales and Dolphins threatened mutual war.
"You must not let it happen as before;
War is not graven by the hand of Fate."

"Your busybody effort lacks effect,"
Said Dolphins. "Where is your authority?
You do not brave the turbulent ocean sea,
So you are no one whom we should respect."

Likewise the Whales: "Oh, Insignificant
Crustacean, why do you insert your presence
Between us and the Dolphins' foul malfeasance?
We might as well take counsel from an Ant."

"Why spurn my gift for mild diplomacy?
Already I have brought you to agree."

Fox and Crab

—AESOP

A Crab decided to desert his beach.
"In this burning stretch of barren hell,
Nothing present but sand and shell,
Every foodstuff is beyond my reach."

A green field lay just past his dune,
So he sidewised there, hoping to dine
On snails and crickets served with wine
Each day of the week precisely at noon.

But sharp-eyed hunger is ever widespread.
Fox spotted Crab in the velvety clover.
"Crustacean," he said, "your short life is over.
I shall eat you at once and be fashionably fed."

"I know I must submit to fate,
Yet shall declare the wisdom I got:
Happy we are when content with our lot."

"Now you are wise, but wise too late."

The Wolf and the Lamb

—LA FONTAINE, I, 10

"Stop fouling the water I must drink,"
Said Wolf. "Whatever made you think
That I'd be willing to forgive
Such injury and let you live
To trouble me another day?"

"I do not comprehend the words you say,"
Replied the inoffensive Lamb.
"Please consider where I am:
Twenty paces below the place
    Where now you quench your thirst.
Water does not flow uphill, Your Grace,
And do recall, you came there first."

"Your defense is no defense;
It makes no slightest difference.
I'm wise to you; I know your game;
Last year you slandered my good name."

"You have confused me with another.
I'm four months old, still nursing from my mother."

"It must have been your brother."
                "I have no brother."

"Well, never mind.
It was some specimen of your kind.
You always threaten with your Dogs and Shepherds,
More fearsome than a jungle full of Leopards.
You plan to murder me and leave no sign;
Before that happens, Vengeance will be mine!"

At this verdict the Lamb, unnerved,
Fell silent. There came to him no words to say.
The Wolf devoured him as his natural prey:
And thus was Justice served.

The Nightingale and the Swallow

—AESOP

Swallow

Why have you become an eremite,
Secluding yourself within this pathless grove
Where the hemlock strains to mount its silhouette
Against the spectral frost-grain of the moon,
To chant of heart-bruise and forsaken love?

Formerly you favored communal life,
The supple give-and-take of gallantry,
The cheerful repartee of man and wife,
The steeple chime that spoke when day was gone,
The ravens gliding to their nightly tree.

You selected from your ancient repertoire
Songs to please both groom and chambermaid,
The mangled soldier bundled home from war,
The widow placing roses by the gravestone,
The mother cradling her infant's fevered head.

Yours, the comforting soliloquy
That welcomed darkness to the drowsy town,
Yours, the liquid, intricate lullaby
That interwove all dreams in unison
Mind to mind until the cloudless dawn.

Now the village copse awaits your song
As the wife awaits her husband's late return
From the weary field he toiled in all day long.
The spinster gazes from her window forlorn;
No nightingale enthralls the slow sundown.

Nightingale

I must not return.
The sorrows of humankind,
Too tearful to be borne,
Disorder my fearful mind.

In the solitude I now inhabit
I shall labor to forget
Things I have heard and seen
In the rude society of men.
Things of which I cannot speak
Without tearful heartbreak.
Hounds are more merciful to wolves
Than men are to themselves.

You swallows gather in a flock
And together you take stock
Of what the villagers do.
You judge with sharp severity
Transgressors of that society,
And censure where the blame is due.
Yet you petition me to bring
At the advent of each evening
Music to transform your world anew.

But I am become a solitary;
My decision will not vary;
Amid these birches I sing alone
Mournful serenades all my own.

Chanson.

Safe within their eternities
Lie the golden Hesperides;
From those Blest Islands the wind bears
Their gift to human years:
The song of the nightingale.

That melody survives
The terms of all the singers' lives;
It abides outside of Time
To be reborn in each of them,
In every individual,
In each nightingale and all.

This the song that Silence would have sung
Had she not vowed never to sing
When she was very young.

The Old Shepherd and the Ass

—AESOP

"Do you not hear the invaders come,
The blaring horn, the incessant drum,
The throb of boots upon the heath,
The clash of weapons bringing death?"
    The elderly Shepherd said,
And in despair hung down his head.
"We the fortunate will find our graves;
All the others will be slaves."

"Yes, I hear their trumpets bray,"
The Ass replied, "and I agree
That our eastern enemy
Will be the masters I obey.
They'll burden me with heavy loads,
Pummel me with wooden rods,
    And feed me moldy hay.
They'll make my life a misery.
I know well how this world goes:
Plus ça change, plus c'est la même-chose."

Paper and Ink

Paper

You track your smoky writhing
Across my pristine surface.
That snaky, dark, and nervous
Defacement you call "writing."
Before your rude intrusion
I was infinite with promise;
Now I am vain surmise,
Dull grammar, glib illusion,
Deceiving the eye and mind
Of gullible humankind.
You violate my essence
With your loquacious presence.
My snowy silence invites
A nobility of thoughts
That when transformed to script
Is weakling and corrupt.

Ink

True, my voluble scribble
Sometimes is merely babble;
Too many phrases are
As empty as the air.
I enunciate sound reason
But also lies and treason.
The qualities of my speech
Must vary each to each
With the hands that set it down.
My mind is not my own,
Occupied by voices
Pronouncing discordant choices.
Without disfiguring Ink
Paper cannot think
And Time lets Paper survive
So that my voices live.

Seeing itself marred by ink's ugly blackness, the paper lodged a complaint.
The ink replied by explaining that the words formed by it were responsible
for the paper being preserved.

—LEONARDO DA VINCI, The Notebooks

The Selfie and the Selfless

To her iPhone app the lady said,
"Now do make me look good!
I'll send this image of my face
Across the instant miles of space
To my dear friend in our old neighborhood."

The app replied to Alma Pride,
"My task is to bear the face you wear
          To whom you want it sent.
To alter its aspects of beauty
Breaches the boundary of my duty
And breaks the terms of our covenant."

"A woman desires to look her best
Any hour of night or day,
By candlelight or digital display.
Every appearance is a test;
In her person or as an image
She always feels herself onstage.
So I petition for your aid,"
The anxious lady said.

"Fulfilling my office, I must do
The duty of a messenger.
Holding me at arm's length, you
Grant yourself a clearer view
Of the Alma that you are.
Are you homely, are you fair?
I don't know and I don't care.
I merely move your face from here to there."

"I had thought our companionship
      Was of a closer nature.
I have spoken more words to you
      Than to any other creature."

"The confidences you let slip
I am wholly indifferent to.
Your concept of the intimate
Is lost upon the inanimate."

"Shall we never establish connection?
Neither warm dislike nor cool affection?
Talking to you is like keeping a tryst
With my bored psychiatrist."

MORAL.

Engage with gadgets and you may find
Few entities are so blankly blind
As an efficient, literal mind.
    Beware a colleague too closely akin
    To the servile, cool machine,
    Because when all is said and done,
    He knows you not and is not known.

The Cock and the Pearl

—LA FONTAINE, I, 20

One day a Cock scratching the ground
Discovered a Pearl perfectly round
And pure, but said with cool disdain,
"I'd value it as a bit of wheat
Or something else cheerful to eat.
Whatever it is won't pass for grain."

We have heard the same derision
Lately voiced by a Politician
Whose motives I shall not describe.
He derogated our Constitution
As an object of cold suspicion:
"It lacks the authority of a Bribe."

Confession

—HORACE, *EPISTLES,* I, II

In one of his Epistles Horace tells
    The tale of Dumbass Rusticus,
        Who curiously had never
        Before encountered a river.
Trickles he'd seen and ditches, little else.
A fellow less informed there hardly was.

    So sat him down he did and waited,
Expecting that the flow would be abated
        As soon as the water drained
From the foggy mountain where it must have rained.
    The current never hesitated;
    Babblingly, bubblingly it ran on
    Long past the hour the sun went down,
Long past the advent of the harvest moon,
Long past the time the winter snows were gone.

    Call it an exercise of will:
    Perhaps our peasant sits there still.

    Two weeks ago I went to hear
    An oration by our Senator.
He promised to unveil a policy
That would make billionaires of you and me.
    He bumbled on and on,
    A bibulous, babbling, baloney drone.
    From phrase to phrase, from clause to clause,
He maundered pointlessly without a pause,
    Gaily, blithely undeterred
    By the actual meaning of any word.

    I listened gamely for one hour plus.
    Call me Dumbass Rusticus.

A Martyr to the Cause

—BABRIUS

A Widow tried to shear
The only Sheep she owned
And, though she took great care,
The clippers often found
The flesh beneath the fleece
With their incisive squeeze.

"Madame, if you recall,
Your husband died last fall
From a Barber's drunken blade
That nigh took off his head.
If you want mutton chop,
Visit a butcher shop.
If fleece is your desire,
Shearsmen are for hire
Whose superior skill
Makes them less apt to kill."

"I do apologize.
My hand is so unsteady
And so tear-dimmed my eyes
I find myself unready
To perform the normal tasks
A normal occasion asks.
I have no money to pay
A shearer to take your wool;
Although my blades are dull,
This chore is mine today.

Please do not shift and squirm
Like an unearthed worm.
Rest easy and behave
As gently as a moth,
So that your painful shave
Transforms to woolen cloth.
When shearing is complete
The both of us shall eat."

"I'll express my gratitude
As I digest the food,
But I shall twitch and bleat
Whenever you draw blood
I will stand patiently
When you stop nipping me.
My patience as a strength
Cannot persist at length.
Now, let us muddle through
This trial of me and you.

MORAL.
  Harsh Necessity
  May breed odd Comity.

Wolf and Crane

—AESOP

Said the exasperated Crane:
"I've every reason to complain.
You agreed to recompense
Me for the inconvenience
Of reaching in and fishing out
The chicken bone lodged in your throat.
Had I not acted as a friend
You would have met a painful end.
Now you can swallow, breathe, and speak,
Thanks to my long slender beak.
We had agreed upon a fee
Which now you have refused to pay.
I do not relish the welsher's joke.
Better had I let you choke."

"I understand your cause for anger.
You bravely saved me from the danger
Of my deadly situation,
A slow and painful strangulation.
But when your head was in my throat
My strongest instinct was to bite.
I exercised great discipline
To let you ease it out again.
Mine is a debt you must forgive.
I paid your fee when I let you live."

MORAL.
Gratitude and courtesy
Will not repay a debtor's fee
Unless you are a savage wolf—
And then of course you will please yourself.

Of Innovation

Said the father Chimpanzee
To his upstart older son,
"Let me show you how it's done:
To gather from the Baobab tree
Do exactly as I do.
Circle round it three times three,
Not four times, and never two;
On count of ten begin the chants
Beseeching Tree's munificence;
At that point the family
Will perform the Harvest Dance
For full six hours and sometimes longer,
And by these means we vanquish hunger."

"I thank you, Father, most gratefully
For your devotion to *history*,
To *custom* and to *ritual*,
But when I go to collect victual,
I simply shimmy up this tree
Tribesmen call a "monkey-bread"
And pluck and eat until I'm fed
And then I slumber peacefully—
Unless the uproar kinfolk make,
Chanting, dancing for *custom's* sake
Is so alarming as to rouse the dead."

"I cannot worship efficiency;
The proven ways that used to be
Have served us well and comfortably.
What if your *shimmy* harmed the wood
And caused the fruit to taste like mud?
If you swing in Baobab trees,

You may contract Arboreal Disease.
A Realist declares it sound
To keep both feet upon the ground."

"Earthbound Realists are grim and drab;
Someone must climb the Baobab.
There should be more to life than what
Once used to be and now is not.
I picture life as a great Perhaps
Wherein my daydreams may collapse
In crumbling ruin upon my head
And leave me broken, so nearly dead
I'll hear the Bugler sounding Taps . . .
Events may turn out otherwise:
I corner trade in monkey-bread,
Control all source of food supplies,
And charge my clients crushing fees.
They'll crown me King of Chimpanzees—
Because I dared to climb the trees."

"Well . . . Pay attention to your Dad;
Always remember what I said.
Many years I've lived and know
Which dreams to follow, which to forego.
What if all we Chimpanzees
Decided to inhabit trees?
Before too long some babbling loon
Would try to *shimmy* to the moon."

Custom, then, is the great guide of human life.
—DAVID HUME, *An Inquiry Concerning
Human Understanding*, V, 1.

The Cat and the Cock

—AESOP

Cock

First, you claim I raise my shrill alarm
    At an unseemly time, in the deep
    Of night when the Man is sound asleep,
Regaining strength for the labors of his farm.

That sleep is necessary, I concede,
Yet if he does not rise an early hour
    It will not be within his power
To till his acres and provide his livestock feed.

Second, you say that I have cruelly attacked
    All who venture near the coop,
    That I knock them down and beat them up.
    I proudly admit that is the fact.

    To protect our Hens by day and night
    Is first of my priorities;
I march the barnyard and I keep the peace
    By showing readiness to fight.

Thirdly, you say my air of arrogance
Annoys the world at large: *Cock of the walk*
Is not a compliment. I've heard such talk,
To me a matter of indifference.

    As a professional I must present
A military bearing, plumage that shows
    Its brassy colors from comb to toes,
    A posture calm, erect, and confident.

Cat

> While listening closely to what you said,
> I pictured hot cracklin' cornbread,
> Boiled potatoes, stewed tomatoes,
> Braised fennel on a lettuce bed,
> And to celebrate our festive day,
> A bright and frisky *brut rosé*.
> Honored as my special guest,
> Seasoned in manner and tastefully dressed,
> And, as the subject of Aesop's fable,
> You're avidly welcome to the table.

MORAL.

*An appetite for argument will never dissuade the
argument of appetite.*

The Cat and the Two Sparrows

—LA FONTAINE, XII, 2

Behaviorists were amused to see
The quick pet Sparrow and the Cat
Engage in harmless duels that
Exercised their friendly rivalry.

The sport continued for years.
The Cat well understood
The bird was not allowable food;
The Sparrow had no fears.

These nimble sparring partners
Inhabited a chateau
And entertained the Maids and Gardeners
With many a mock set-to.

Their range of acquaintance was narrow;
Cat imagined his feathered friend
The same as every other Sparrow
All the world around.

But one unfortunate day
A window was left ajar
And a stranger Sparrow entered from far
Away.

This unknown interloper
Was very rude indeed;
He had no notion of what was proper
And what was not allowed.

He fluttered chirping about the house,
  Through bedrooms, pantries, hallways,
Leaving each a dreadful mess
  And taunting Cat always.

Fuzzbutt, he called him, The Big-Eyed Wonder,
And Creepabout and Pillowdozer,
Old Spooky Slinker, Nature's Blunder,
  And Mouseless Mouser.

Down he swooped upon the Cat
  And flittered at his nose,
Ever careful to estimate
The stretched extension of his paws.

One luckless hour he miscalculated
His necessary certain distance
And met the end for which he was fated,
  A sad instructive instance.

Cat gulped him down with a thankful growl;
  In a speculative mood
He studied how any creature so vile
  Was flavored so darn good.

He began at length to ponder
The Wherefores and the Whys
And gazed upon his dear playmate with wonder
  And strange surmise.

The Lion and the Melodious Ass

—LA FONTAINE, II, 19

A Lion, celebrating his birthday,
Scouted through the broad landscape for prey,
Rejecting any scrawny, piddling meal
To feed on venison, wild boar, and veal.
Leo owns a noble appetite
And will not squander it on puny, bite-
Sized Chickadee, Chipmunk, or Butterfly,
Cute canapes that do not satisfy.

But when he prowled into the intricate wood,
No mammals introduced themselves as food,
Although they were about. He felt the presence
Of Woodchuck, Hare, and Boar, and smelled their essence,
But lattices of sunlight in the glade
Hid them as thoroughly as deepest shade,
And den, briar patch, and thicket brake
Helped them avoid becoming Tartar steak.
"Some means must be devised to flush him from
The leafy nook where Roebuck makes his home.
If now the Preservation Hall Jazz Band
Would shake the forest with its jubilee sound,
The Buck and Doe would show themselves at once,
Fleeing the uproar—or prancing out to dance."
He searched his memory to recollect
Those sounds that make a shattering impact:
Bagpipes, Schoenberg, heavy metal rock,
The organ toccata of J. Sebastian Bach,
Avalanches crushing mountain passes,
The passionate commotion of mating Asses.

The Lion now recalled his pal Beaulane,
Uproarious Wild Ass tenor of the plain,
Who often proved a stout companion
For drinking parties and racier types of fun.

"Beaulane, my friend! Are you in voice today,
Ready to yodel, run the scales, and bray?
I have conceived a twilight japery
To bring acclaim to you and food to me.
Do you remember how last New Year's Eve
You thrilled us all by singing 'I Believe,'
'A Wand'ring Minstrel I,' and 'Summertime'?
We toasted your renditions as sublime.
I have discovered a fledgling audience,
Shy, but eager to experience
Music of the operatic kind,
Inventive, learned, sensual, and refined.
If you will come at moonrise to Arden Grove
And give your stirring version of 'Be My Love,'
I guarantee you'll get the huge response
That for most artists happens only once."

The Ass replied, "I'll be there. Cross my heart."
Debating with a Lion isn't smart,
He thought, *and where's the harm in a refrain
Of 'Ridi, Pagliaccio' or 'Singin' in the Rain'?
It profits me to stand in his good graces
And gain advantage over other Asses.*

The Lion's raucous plan was executed:
By Arden Grove the Ass heehawed and hooted;

Seven galloping animals broke cover,
Visceral panic being a primal mover.
Gory remnants lay scattered on the ground
Because of Ass's terrifying sound.

"I have performed the favor you required.
Now, what may I expect as my reward?"

"These horns and ears disposed about the glade
Are yours, as fee for one who merely brayed."

"This nasty ordure? Lion, never again
Shall you engage the labors of Beaulane.
I was deceived, hoping you'd be fair.
But Lion always grabs the Lion's share."

"You say you are displeased. I do not doubt it.
The question is, What will you do about it?
I think no matter what you say or do,
Your character as an Ass shows through."

MORAL.
"Know thyself." *Socrates*
Shines true throughout the centuries.
If you're an Ass, own up to it;
No grander title will ever fit;
When you pretend to something more,
You're a bigger Ass than you were before.

The Serpent's Head and the Tail

—LA FONTAINE, VIII, 16

Tail

The arrangement in place is grossly unjust:
You breathe clean air, I breathe your dust;
With every forward motion you
Find an enlightening fresh view;
I sadly stultify my mind,
Reviewing what we leave behind;
If we continue in this state,
Mine shall be a dismal fate.

Head

The situation *is* unfair.
Do not imagine I do not care,
But it is useless to complain
Unless you formulate a plan.

Tail

Very often I have thought,
If only we could switch about,
Exchanging both our present stations,
Simply reversing situations,
So that I, the Tail, would lead,
To be followed by the Head,
A happy balance would be struck;
You could enjoy the backward look,
Confirming the proverb we all know:
"Hindsight is the certain view."

Head

I suppose it only fair
That our positions we should share.
But is it wise to undertake
Novelty for its own sake?
Many noble experiments
Result in ruinous consequence,
And many are those who sought relief
Only to bring themselves to grief.

Head's fears proved true;
All went askew.
Tail found to its surprise
Foresight requires the use of eyes.

Let us not bother to recount
The blunders that now the Serpent made;
They totaled to a vast amount:
So, when all is done and said,
We find that always, without fail
It is imprudent to assign your tail
The duties of your head.

Wolf and Shepherds

—LA FONTAINE, X, V

"I am the common enemy of all,
            Outcast hated by everyone
            From watchful sire to youngest son.
There is none whom I do not appall.
And so they set on me, the hunstmen, hounds,
            And villagers. The land resounds
                        With baying of pursuit;
                              All the counties
                              Have posted bounties
            In every place I print my foot,"
Said the solitary Wolf
                        To his lonesome self.

            "True, I sometimes prey on sheep,
                  The infirm, old, or lame.
            When the Shepherd does not keep
Dutifully alert and falls asleep
                        While his flock grazes
                  The brushy mountain passes,
            I consider them fair game.
            I am reputed Monster because
            I am obedient to natural laws.
            Maybe I'll change my cast of mind
And alter my essential character;
Perhaps if I behave like Humankind,
            I shan't be named a murderer
            But welcomed in society
            As one whose dietary reform
            Eliminates cause for alarm.
I'll be a model of propriety—

"But what is that unseemly noise?
And who are those unruly boys?"

"Pepper, mustard, cool mint jam,
These are spices fit for lamb!
Beef is good and so is ham,
But the only best is lamb!
Lads, to make it more divine,
We'll sluice it down with tubs of wine!"

"If I may trust my eyes,
I'm sure I recognize
Many members of this rowdy crowd
As they swill and shout and dance
And bellow rude, bloodthirsty chants
In voices much too loud.

"There goes Colin. Is that Damian?
I spot Linus and Corydon.
I know these Shepherds every one.
What motivates this bacchanal?
Their rioting brings shame on all
Their pastoral vocation.
Around the flames they leap and dance
Like Maenads in god-maddened trance."

"Fetch me lamb to fricasee
And you will make a friend of me!
My pal Thyrsis savors most
A tender, smoking loin roast!
Chops are tasty, so is stew,
But best of all is barbecue!"

"Commingled with the smoke,
A scent arises that intoxicates
My mind. It marries with the fume of oak,
        Drawing my soul to higher states
        Of consciousness. What kind of meat
        Do they revolve upon that spit?"

"No broccoli, no candied yam—
All we want to eat is lamb!
Bring us whiskey by the dram
Because it goes so well with lamb!
Delicious child of Ewe and Ram,
We adore the juicy lamb!"

"Do my bewildered eyes deceive?
—Yet what I see I must believe.
The animal that is the Shepherds' care
        Furnishes the flesh they tear.
They celebrate their orgiastic rite
        By feasting on forbidden meat
And when the savage ritual is done
        They go to hunt the Wolf again,
        Each a perfect hypocrite.

"I'll find a mountain stream to cleanse me free
Of the least suggestion of Humanity.
        Nobler to be an animal
        Than a two-faced criminal."

The Cat and the Birds

—AESOP

Cat

Good morning, Madam. May I present
My card? I'm proud to represent
The agency of Tallon Clawe,
Health Insurance Attorneys-at-Law.
We furnish the finest legal minds
To clients of all feathered kinds.
We study every circumstance;
Nothing whatever is left to chance.
Our source we're not allowed to mention,
But notice comes to our attention
That you should be extremely wary
Here in your cozy Aviary.
It's rumored that your Cockatoo
Has caught a touch of avian flu
The Robin reported late last night
The onslaught of a pernicious mite;
And this cruel, early freeze
Delivered the Crow a nasty sneeze.
To prevent worse future infection
I should make a full inspection;
Allow me to investigate
And I will leave you a clean slate.

Parrot

How bold of you to come today!
Felines generally stay away,
Apprehensive of the scowl
Of our watchful Great Horned Owl,
Who tells me that he favors Cat
For the eyeballs and the fat.
Our premises are most hygienic,
As clean as any standard clinic,
And our "cozy Aviary"
Employs a licensed Actuary
Whose specialty of expertise is
Tracing transmittable diseases.
He can predict all possible harm
Engendered by the wayward germ.
Now, for discussion of matters legal
I shall acquaint you with our Eagle,
Who, though he relishes a tort,
Prefers to settle out of court.
Eager to aid your delegates,
He'll guide them to the Pearly Gates. . .
It seems that of the things you sell
We have no need. Goodbye. Farewell.

MORAL.
If you like your health plan, you should keep your health plan.

The Wolf, the Fox, and the Ape

—AESOP

Wolf

"No, Your Honor, I did not see
This villain steal my food from me,
But all the pawprints about the larder
Obviously belong to Reynard or
One who matches his shape and weight
           Precisely.
There was besides more than a hint
Of his detestable vulpine scent,
Mingled with spray of an alley cat.
Perhaps he engaged a confederate,
Or had enlisted more than three
Henchmen in his strategy
           Unwisely.
When you consider the evidence
I'm sure you'll find he lacks a defense
And all the lamb shanks heaped in his den
Should be restored to me again."

Fox

"Your Honor, these charges are absurd.
No sane being credits Wolf's word
In any matter where verity
Stands as a firm necessity.
In my house I was frying bacon
When these fictitious shanks were taken,
           As per his claim.
My faithful spouse will testify
That long past midnight she and I
Had been reciting Bible verses
And planning how to tender mercies

To many poor unfortunates,
As rule of Charity dictates
                    In Our Savior's name.
So, I have penned a proclamation
Against Wolf's lurid defamation
Of my trustworthy character
And now request its approval here."

Ape
"This is the last case I will hear
Before my retirement late this year.
I've weighed both causes and, I must say,
I wish I could un-bench today.
You the Wolf sue for the loss
Of a cut of lamb that never was,
                    A transparent fraud.
And you the Fox did brazenly steal
Said lamb to make an illicit meal.
We often hear the proverb, *Sly*
As a Fox, and know the reason why.
On this and every other occasion
You are preceded by your reputation,
                    Worse than bad.
To these proceedings I call a halt
By finding both of you at fault,
Set each of you a sizable fine—
Which in sum total shall be mine.

MORAL.
Justice *and* Law *are not synonyms.*

The Lion, the Wolf, and the Fox

—AESOP

Said Wolf to Lion: "I will not deny,
O King, that Fox and I have fallen out
Sometimes, for reasons largely misconstrued
By our fellow citizens of the wood.
They were misled by an ingenious lie
That Fox invented and widely spread about.

"For instance, he once told the Judge that I
Broke into his home and stole a cut
Of lamb . . . Sire, that lamb did not exist.
Yet even so, the rumor will persist
Because he skews the facts so skillfully,
Though I hold evidence he can't rebut.

"Our most combative topic of contention
Was in the matter of his loyalty.
Had you intelligence which came to me,
You would share my apprehension.
Was he candid when he bared his soul
To you, or was it one more foxy tale?

"We, your loving subjects, are distressed
To learn of serious illness that afflicts
Our King. We have consulted with the best
Of all the palace doctors and he expects
A vast improvement to take begin quite soon.
Meanwhile, the Fox is nowhere to be seen."

"Are *you* an upright paragon, Squire Wolf?"
The Lion asked. "I hear it said you thieve,
Maraud, and feed upon the helpless flocks
Our Shepherds guard. How shall I believe
Your slipshod accusations against the Fox?
He entered as you spoke . . . Ask him yourself."

"For my brief absence I beg your Royal pardon,"
Said Fox, as he came forward with a bow.
"Your illness must bear a disruptive burden.
I looked about for means to alleviate
The pains distracting you from affairs of state
And found a Healer certain he knows how.

"His skill is such that you once decorated
His chest with medals he richly merited.
A change of diet will easily restore,
He said, the health that you enjoyed before.
With your permission, I will go myself
To pass the Healer's notions to your chef."

"Let me inspect the list of ingredients
To ascertain what I can tolerate.
I have a pronounced allergy to quince
And always relish meat upon my plate.
What does he prescribe in way of food?
—*Fricasee of Wolf?* Oh that sounds good."

Truce

The Cat Ignatius, green-eyed and deeply sable,
Is guardian of this lowly wayside stable.
From his rafter he watchfully beholds
As the bright Nativity below unfolds.

Here are the Mother and her shining Son,
Here, Joseph in rapt wonder looking on;
Gaspar, Melchior, and Balthasar
Offering gold and frankincense and myrrh.
Three shepherds enter from the starry field
To witness presentation of the Child,
Guided by a sphere of ardent light
That casts a silver silence on the night.

All is always as it should have been
To fix in reverence this eternal scene—
Except for gangs of drunken rats that race
Hither, yonder, all across the space,
Scrambling and quarreling. They squeak, squeal, and chitter,
And make a gruesome mess in palm-straw litter.
Their behavior is a sickening disgrace
As welcome for the infant prince of peace.

Ignatius is displeased. He could descend
To deal them each a just and sudden end;
But this one night his duty is to forgive.
Besides, he knows their names and where they live.

Doctor Wolf

—BABRIUS

"The Wolf is stalking me,"
Thought the wary Ass.
"I shall pretend to be
Preoccupied with grass,
But every now and then
I'll bray as if in pain
And I shall lay me down
With a pitiable moan."

"I think I know just how you feel:
The same as I, were I the meal
Of a clever, hungry predator
Certain he knows what Asses are for."

"I bow to destiny.
It is inevitable
That I am edible,
A common calamity.
My immediate source of torment
Is of greater moment:
A thorn lodged in my shin
Causes atrocious pain,
And so I bray untunefully.
For your own benefit
You must draw it out.
Come closer, closer now;
Extend your skillful jaw."

!!!!

"What a villainous dirty trick!
You gave my snout a monstrous kick!
You broke five teeth, and what is more,
You made my face a running sore;
You blacked my eyes and smashed my nose
With your ill-mannered, treacherous blows.
You've done what none, or very few,
True-bred gentlemen would do."

"In this one lucky hour
I possessed the power
Of prudent self-defense.
In half an hour hence
You surely would devour
This Ass from head to tail
And my four hooves as well.
To strike a defensive blow
Is honorable to do."

"I have discovered something new:
Merely because I have learned to kill
And am allowed to go scot-free
Does not confer me surgical skill
Or medical degree.
Who am I to sew a suture?
I was born to be a butcher."

The Soothsayers

—AESOP

Apollo

I thank you each for your polite response
     To my summons to address
     Questions about the prophetess
Sibylla and the seer Pancrates
     That have perplexed me more than once.

Horse

My presence here before the god I serve
     Is honor I do not deserve.

Ass

I have followed and will always follow
     The measures of the god Apollo.

Apollo

They could never be more different,
     These two figures who present
Themselves as able to foretell
     What lies in store for wealthy clients
     Who recompense them extremely well
        To break their golden silence.

You consult Sibylla faithfully,
     Strider. Tell us why.
Do the outcomes she reveals to you
     Always come true?

Horse

Almost all.
It has been a grand surprise
How conformably her prophecies
In time befall.
Some eventualities
She will not disclose:
The hour of my death, that of my wife,
And what will happen in the afterlife
To my equine soul.
Otherwise, what she avers
Almost always occurs.

Apollo

You find no need of careful correction
In her powers of prediction?

Horse

I enjoy reliable success
In a final analysis.
Sometimes an outcome is effected
When I least expect it;
Sometimes events get out of hand
Because I fail to understand.
Yet her insight as oracle
Is nigh a miracle.

Apollo

Plodlow, do you find
Accuracy of an equal kind

In your audiences
With the soothsayer Pancrates?
A rumor is abroad
That his clairvoyant powers are hit-or-miss,
That he has erred in half the things he said,
And once was formally accused of fraud.

Ass

Farshooter, I'll keep it short:
Accuracy is not his forte.
Sometimes episodes unfold
As Pancrates foretold,
But there are other instances
When he strays by immense distances.
Often he comes fairly near
To seeing clear,
But just as often he
Fails spectacularly.

Apollo

Why then, Plodlow, would you take heed
Of anything he ever said?
Would it not be sensible
And more thrifty
To let your future time itself unveil?
Your chances will be fifty-fifty
Lacking Pancrates to tell the tale.
In the matter of unearthing
The future, why not listen to the sure thing?
Strider has testified
His prophetess is bona fide.

Ass

If I were Horse
I would follow his blessed course.
But I am Ass,
Belonging to a different class
Of mortal being
And I prefer a mistier foreseeing.

If Sybilla says
The Horse will win the half-mile race,
Thus will it come to pass.
If Pancrates predicts that I
Will win, I listen doubtfully,
But in that moment, in my mind's eye.
I see the maidens enwreathe my ears
With garlands while the wild crowd cheers
Plodlow! with one voice—
A most gratifying noise.

Apollo

But this triumph did not take place.
You lost the race
That Strider won
To his lasting fame.

Ass

The winner has to run it ever the same.
I clopped the race course one time only,
So far behind friend Strider I felt lonely.
But in my mind I beheld the scene
As it might have been
If my makeup were of alternate kind:
Fleet of physique instead of mind.

I reached the finish some time after
Strider, to the sounds of cruel laughter.
                    O yes, I lost the race
Foretold as victory by Pancrates
                    In his delusive prophecies;
                    But in my mind a double race
                    Occurred, and I competed twice.
                    One race was a victory
                              That only I could see.

Apollo

                    But actually you know
                    That vision was untrue.
                    You are unwelcome in the halls
                    Of victors. The prophecy was false.

Ass

                    What you say is indeed the case
And yet, false hope enabled me to race.
                    Without Illusion to believe
                    I would not care to live.

The Horse and the Soldier

—AESOP

In time of peace the Horse
Recalled those warrior years
When his hefty master Knight
Rode abroad to fight
With an army of brave men
The eastern Saracen.

He bore Sir Wotless daily
Into battle, gaily
Accoutered with sword and spear
And other clankerous gear.
The burden of the Knight
Demanded all his might;
If he were not well foddered,
The warhorse would have tottered
And buckled to the soil
To become sad enemy spoil.

So he was provided oats,
Sally grass and groats,
Sufficient barley meal
And hearty barley ale.
All this stalwart victual
Maintained the horse's mettle
So he withstood onslaught
Of infantry when he fought.

At last the crusade ended
And a sullen peace descended.
When Wotless returned to farm
He did a shameful harm

To his faithful veteran mount
Who now received but scant
And tasteless, puny nutrition
For his most meager ration.

He sledded oafish loads
Along the muddy roads,
His present life a story
Without a gleam of glory;
His days all fell together,
Each one like the other.
His gallant fortitude
Fell into desuetude.

But do wars ever cease?
There came an end to peace.
Some King or restless Prince
Decided to take offense
Concerning a minor disorder
On one or the other border.
Generals took the field,
Vowing never to yield.

Sir Wotless saddled his steed
With a humbling lack of speed,
But when he dug his spur
The horse refused to stir.
"The treatment I receive
Since last I took my leave
From the clash of soldiery
Now quite disables me.
No longer have I strength

To gallop the bloody length
Of a smoking battleground
At the bugle's urgent sound.
Ragweed and briars for food
Impair the martial mood.
You saved a paltry cost
To find your cause is lost."

MORAL.
Against a setting sun
The dispirited veteran
Imposes a silhouette
Memory strives to blot.
For shelter and for food
He receives ingratitude,
For bravery in wars,
His only medals the scars.

The Sickly Stag

—LA FONTAINE, XII, 6

In a savannah where Deer were plentiful
   A Stag fell deathly ill.
  A dozen other Stags came round
  To comfort and to sympathize.
  In those last hours new friends abound
   When a lonely elder dies.

  "Gentles, let me pass in peace;
  In solitude my life should cease.
  Please omit the shopworn, phony
  Bromides and empty ceremony
   So that my fatal day
   Can gracefully display
  Some modest sign of dignity."

No such luck. The entourage kept near,
  Grazing his territory clear
  Of leaf and rush, of grass and bush,
Of any verdure that might feed this Deer.
Our ailing Stag would have to travel far
  To find so much as a cockleburr.
  Lacking solid nourishment,
He succumbed quietly to perishment.

  MORAL.
 Tend well your liver, spleen, and gizzard,
   For at the end
   Your every friend
  May play the role of Buzzard.

The Old Man and His Grandson

—GRIMM'S FAIRY TALES, 363

Little Hans was shaping a mold
And lining it with strips of wood,
Joining these as best he could.
Little Hans was eight years old.

His puzzled parents queried Hans,
Who seemed to have developed plans,
Concerning the purpose of his work.

"Oh, do you not recall the days
Grandfather sat with us at table,
Before he lost his piercing gaze,
Before his palsy made him unable
Firmly to grasp his knife and fork?"

"But he was likely to spill his broth
Across our finest tablecloth,"
His father said. His mother complained
The elder's trousers were often stained.

"You made him sit in the corner there
Like discarded furniture
And eat from a bowl of earthenware."

"He dropped that bowl upon the floor.
The pieces scattered everywhere."

"Then you ordered a bowl of wood
Which spoiled the taste of his scanty food.
So I am building an oaken trough

That surely will be grand enough
For you to sup from when you're old.
—When you object, oh how I'll scold!"

The father then hung down his head
And to his blushing wife he said,
"Our son is wiser than we are;
Your dad deserves our utmost care.
Old age is never cause for blame;
Despising Ned earns us deep shame.
We shall restore his honored seat
And give him caviar to eat."

The Lion Grown Old

—LA FONTAINE, III, 14

Lion, now that he was ancient,
Became a target of attack
By subjects vengeful and impatient.
Horse came by to present a kick
Where Leo sheltered in his den;
Wolf arrived to award a bite
After inquiring, "*Remember when?*
This time I shan't lose the fight."
Ox administered, as once before,
A profoundly painful double gore;
Then to conclude that hour of woe
Ass gave Lion his fatal blow.

Lion muttered with his last breath,
"Death by Ass is twice a death."

PSYCHOLOGY

The Eagle, the Cat, and the Wild Sow

—AESOP

Chapter One

Cat, to her Kittens Three

It was a lucky day
When I discovered the hole
In this legendary White Oak trunk
Where bachelor Opossum used to bunk
Till loneliness engulfed his soul
And he moved away.
I thought this ancient tree
Seemed to welcome me
To settle in and birth you three,
My Wispy, my Pipsy, and my Hermione.

How snug and safe it seems until you know
Atop an Eagle houses, and below,
Tusking at the roots, is a Wild Sow.
This urgent information
Casts somber light upon the situation;
Yet my ambition is to share with none.
This Oak must shelter us alone,
Though gaining dominion of this Tree
Demands complex diplomacy.

Chapter Two

Cat, to the Eagle

My thanks for granting audience
On this day busy for one and all!
Because you, as our sentinel,
Maintain a constant vigilance,
I clawed my way up here to tell
You of a peril you may not know:
The footing of our security

Is being subverted even now
By a malevolent Wild Sow
And her filthy Piglets Three.

Have you not noticed in wild weather
How our domicile tree behaves?
It thrashes like an otter on a tether,
Or dinghy rocked in rampant waves.
For safety we must join together.

If Sow continues excavating,
Down comes Oak, Eaglets, and all.
We must cause fear in her brute soul;
I will inform her you are waiting
To pay a ravenous house call.

So, if you stand watch faithfully
On a leafless limb where she can see,
She will not stray from the sheltering bole,
Anxious to guard her Piglets Three—
And the four will starve in their hidey-hole.

Our homes will then be safe and sound
Where songbirds, rodents, and snakes abound;
The ferocious Sow will never destroy
Our Tree's deep network in the ground
And wither all our future joy.

Chapter Three

Cat, to Her Kittens

Now I have arranged the matter so
The Eagle will not leave her sentry bough
   But steadfastly observe the Sow
   And everything she does below.

We four will go abroad tonight
　　　　To hunt for Mice and Moles,
　　　　　Brisk Chipmunks and swift Voles,
And stock our pantry till the shelves are tight.
　　　　But when we go abroad by day
　　　　We'll peer about us every way,
As if we lived each hour in mortal fright;
　　　　　And this is how
We shall deceive both Eagle and Wild Sow.

My pressing duty is to oversee
　　　　The safety of my Kittens Three,
You Wispy, you Pipsy, and you, Hermione.

Chapter Four
Cat, to Wild Sow

Missus Sow, I much admire
The way you diligently dig
To extend your housing in the mire.
Were I equipped, I might aspire
To ape your example as a Pig.

But both of us are being watched;
Sinister schemes are being hatched;
All our movements are observed.
I feel that we will be ill-served
And our projects will be scotched.

My apprehensions are not groundless.
I have seen the shadow of
A giant raptor perched above.
Who knows when he will make his move?
The evils of this world are boundless.

I am not one to thrust advice
Upon my friends I know are wise,
But have you noticed how your Piglets
Adore to frolic in the thickets,
Scrambling about like merry Mice?

For the Eagle, tempting prey.
Is it prudent to let them stray
About the landscape as they will?
In time this peril must pass away,
Till then, the Eagle means to kill.

Chapter Five

Cat, to Her Kittens

Let us begin the game of Patience.
It is arranged so Eagle and Sow
Will never plot to harm us now.
In both of them I provoked such fear
They dare not forage anywhere.

We have sufficient store of rations;
    If we lie calm and wait,
Certain starvation is their fate.
We shall enjoy our feeless lease
    And live our lives in peace.

MORAL.

Cats are cunning. This we know
For the Fables tell us so.
If Fables were vain Fantasy,
They would not live in memory,
Reminding us forevermore
Of the kinds of animals we are.

The Wolf and the Dove Gathering Twigs

—AESOP

Wolf

Why do you skirmish all around
To gather twigs from the forest ground?
Toward what goal do you aspire?
I've never seen you build a fire,
Nor is your homeplace made of wood.
Pray tell me, Madame, for what good?

Dove

A dozen sheep I've seen you raid
With only your own mouth to feed,
Nor have I seen you wearing tweed.
Sir Lupus, won't you please confide,
Is it from hunger or from greed
That you can need more than you need?

The Two Frogs

—AESOP

"Come live near me and be my friend,"
The Pond Frog to the Puddle Frog said.
"You shall see how the tasteful moon
Adorns with platinum my lagoon,
Observe how gracefully the wind
Causes the slender reeds to bend,
As if each individual sway
Was part of midnight's grand ballet
Performed until the stars are fled."

"But I am perfectly satisfied,"
The Puddle Frog to the Pond Frog said,
"With the humble life that now I lead
Here in the mud of a rutted road.
I catch a glimpse of society
When haughty carriages pass me by—"

His exposition was rendered short
By the sightless wheels of a rumbling cart.

If only my friend had understood,
Pond Frog considered with heavy heart,
The potent perils of lowly mud
We could still gossip and disport.

The Bald Man and the Fly

—PHAEDRUS

Have you ever seen a Mosquito laugh?
  —A manifestation closely local,
    Gestural and never vocal,
    A bitsy hitch in its midflight,
    A visual effect extremely slight,
    Like a tiny freckle on a giraffe.

    If you had witnessed the episode
    When the Insect bit a Man's bald head
    You would have seen how the fellow smote
    Resoundingly his naked pate
    And heard the words Mosquito said:

        "Mon vieux, your estimate
        Of the power I possess
        Is flattering indeed;
        I could not raise a bruise
        On your delicious head
        In drawing my mite of blood.
    You slapped your scalp, trying to slaughter
    A foe the size of a drop of water."

        "Easily I forgive
        Myself the injury
        Accidentally
        Inflicted. I believe
        That only an act malicious
        Can be considered vicious.
    Did you not spend a sleepless night
    Planning how to deliver your bite?"

"The imperative to feed
Is an undeniable need.
A sudden hungriness
Convinced me I should zizz
Above your fulgent dome,
To dine and quickly zoom.
I have no reason to harm you
No motive to alarm you,
But for the frisson of joy
When I choose to annoy.
You did yourself more damage
Than I could ever manage.
Your shiny scalp is a beacon signal
To the deft Mosquito who enjoys a giggle."

Angel and the Knot of Vipers

Dozing Angel abruptly awakes
As his mistress steps into a nest of snakes.
Fired with instinct to protect,
With ears laid flat and tail erect,
He attacks them furiously, bites and gnaws,
And rends them pitiably with his claws.

"Angel! You've ruined my new shoelaces!
You must teach yourself to distinguish species!"

The chastened youngster creeps away to hide
And nurse the remnants of his pride,
Hoping to calm the impatient mood
Of the Lady who brings him punctual food.
He ponders how to classify
The different creatures that meet his eye.

MORAL.

To prevent all similar occurrence,
Learn not to judge from mere appearance.
All things that slither from a hole
Are not of serpentine condition:
Recall the Redworm and the Mole
                    And the slimy Politician.

Of Extortion

—GESTA ROMANORUM, LI

"Senator Guano, you're known by all
As one corrupt and prodigal;
You rashly glutton and overimbibe,
You hear no citizen without a bribe;
The air is heavy with the pigsty smell
Of the hundred thousand lies you tell,
Lies so gross they take the shapes
Of the fecal matter of Barbary Apes.
Frantic, bombastic, ignorant, vain—
Yet we elect you again and again."

"My friends, your tone is bracingly frank.
I'll take a solemn moment to thank
All my supporters. To you I owe
The fortune I own and the tricks I know.
I'm tolerant when you criticize,
Reminding me I am no prize,
Since when you enter the voting booth
You put aside concern for truth.
Though I may be a civic curse,
You have imagined someone worse,
A Statesman honest, wise, and just,
Fully deserving the public trust,
One on whom the oppressed may call,
A figure not like yourselves at all.
You who support my candidacy

Find likeness of yourselves in me,
A man to whom you feel akin,
Immersed in shame, expert in sin.
Let the Moralists preach and prate—
No seat is safer than my seat."

MORAL.

The people heaved a dark, collective sigh
And stood by Guano. And so did I.

Fly

—FRANCIS BACON, "OF VAINGLORY"

"Here I come to save the day!
Mighty Fly will show the way!
Lesser insects must beware
When Mighty Fly patrols the air!"

After this proud boast Musca the Fly
    Felt his energies deplete.
He thought to hitch a ride on a farmer's cart.
    "I see no enemy nearby
    It is my duty to defeat
By means of strategy or martial art.
Here's opportunity to take a breather
From zooming the insubstantial aether,
On the lookout everywhere I go
    For an estimable foe."

He settled on the sternward end to view
The summer landscape he was rolling through
But found his sight obstructed by a cloud
Of dingy powder lifting from the road.

"My wondrousness has grown beyond all praise.
Behold the monumental dust I raise!"

The Lion Defeated by a Man

—LA FONTAINE, III, 10

"Excuse me, please. I was strolling by
When this painting caught my eye,
Presenting with bold simplicity
A silly, naive mythology.
This image from a childish mind
Was rendered by an arrogant hand."

Thus the critical Lion addressed
A group of gawkers so impressed
By the garish artwork on display
They were reluctant to turn away.

"Here your cunning Artist drew
A hunter no Lion ever knew,
A Human of surpassing brawn
Who all alone brought Lion down.
His foot upon the Lion's corpus
Portrays him as a Man of purpose;
The haughty brandishment of his spear
Signals to all his lack of fear;
His tight-lipped, cruel, triumphant smirk
Trumpets pride in his dirty work.

"But view the world through a different prism;
Go visit the School of Realism:
There the Man in Lion combat
Fares no better than a Wombat;
Lion swats Man with a mighty paw
Producing a feeling of painful awe;
He drags him to a shady place

To rip the features from his face;
At last he fixes the fate of him
By separating limb from limb.
A Realist Artist carefully paints
The correct details of true events.
See great Leo gnaw Man's heart
In the Lion Museum of Classical Art."

Motivation

—HORACE, *EPISTLES*, II, II

Corporal Boff was well and truly pissed.
Someone stole belongings he had stored
In his foot locker. He'd heaped no bulging hoard,
    But he had won an amethyst
Of pinkish purple that he felt would suit
    His darling Jinx because her eyes
In a certain cast of expensive candle light
    Seemed to emit expressive violet rays.

He cursed himself and all divinities.
    No one dared to cross his path
For fear the grim volcano of his wrath
    Would render them to bone and grease.
So when his company was ordered out
    To take an outpost garrison
The corporal voiced a terrifying shout,
    Attacking the fort, one man alone.

The chroniclers describe the glorious deed
    In glorious terms. Singlehand,
He captured the post, took down the flag, and freed
    The prisoners. Against all orders
    He then ransacked the commander's quarters
Where he discovered a trove of contraband:
Three diamonds of the very finest waters,
Eight gold bangles, and some Cannabis seed.

Grand ceremonies followed thereupon,
Complete with speeches and coruscant medal.
Corporal Boff withstood this proud ordeal
And, when it ended, instantly was gone.

But now came Captain Bugle with a plan
For Boff to seize another garrison.
                    "Child's play for such a man
As you. This time you needn't fight alone."

"I thank you for the opportunity.
Some other day I might accept the dare,
But Jinx consented to be my fiancée
With all the glitter she could ever wear.
Search, Sir, and you will find another bloke
Whose luck has turned and left him stony broke,
Some raw jughead whose girl kissed him goodbye,
So all he does is drink the strip joints dry."

Shepherd and Hound

—BABRIUS

"Friend Hermes, you are growing old.
You used to be the fastest Hound
The Kennel Master ever found,"
Said graybeard Colin by his sheepfold.
"Your hot pursuit of Cottontail
Was sweetly rewarded without fail,
But now you have acquired a habit
Of straggling home without a Rabbit,
    So I am told."

Hermes replied, "It may be true
That I have lost a step or two,
But Lion has it in for me
And if it's speed you like to see
I can achieve a moderate haste.
My more heroic velocity
Returns when I myself am chased.
I leave my trail a scorching track
With hungry Leo at my back:
There is no stronger motivation
Than the Lion's salivation,
And to avoid his unkindly bite,
I might outpace the speed of light."

MORAL.

To attain an impressive speed
Sometimes requires a pressing need.

The Bear and the Gardener

—LA FONTAINE, VIII, 10

Loneliness drove the Bear
From his abode on the brushy mountain;
Vigilance drew the Gardener
From greensward flowers and burbling fountain.

They wandered at random from place to place,
Gardener and Bear,
Until they encountered face to face
In a public square.

And so opened an episode
Strange in the records of mammalian kind:
No grisly conflict fangsome and crude
But companionship of mind and mind.

The subjects that they struck upon
When they began to speak
Were of shrubs that lavished in full sun
And mosses smoothing rocks beside a creek.

Of laurels, coltsfoot, chamomile,
And thistles floating on the breeze,
They could converse for an endless while
As avid devotees.

When Gardener inquired about the strain
Of Rose preferred by his new companion,
Bear found it awkward to explain
That Rose of any sort he had never seen.

"From such report as I have heard
Roses all other blooms surpass.
So say the Field Mouse, the petite Bluebird,
And the briar-munching Ass.

"The colors, they say, are delicate pearl
Or red as the passionate blood
Of yearning lad and smitten girl
Dreaming a-bed.

"Sometimes the Rose is gold, they say,
Sometimes so perfectly white
It will hide itself from the sun by day
And embrace the moon at night.

"So, if I never see this flower
My life continues incomplete."
"And that is why," said the Gardener,
"I've led us to my garden gate."

He sprang the lock and shot the bolt
And opened wide the portal;
Bear lurched in and looked about and felt
He entered a Bower of the Immortal.

Such were the beauties of the *Lady Grace,*
The *Lady Banks,* the *Eglantyne,*
Mme. de Armandière, Dulcet Beatrice,
The shy *Princesse Helene,*

The *Dalilah,* the *Princesse Eugenia,*
The *Duchesse de Brabant,* the *Angel Breath,*
The Holy Rose of Abyssinia,
The *Susan Elizabeth.*

The roseate splendor overwhelmed him quite;
     His world spun wildly. On the lush lawn
     He sat him down to absorb the sight
That filled his spirit like the ascent of dawn.

     No sooner had he begun to praise
     Each specimen for its special glory
Than the Gardener descanted upon a Rose
That sprang in a land distant and legendary:

     The Rose *Roxane*. Alexander the Great
     Had demanded from his Floralist
A bloom to symbolize, in bridal state,
A Beauty that once existed and ever will exist.

     It flourishes within a mysterious isle
Off the eastern coast of India where
     Potentialities all minds beguile
And the Ideal embodies its particular.

     There Visions become material,
     Conferring Dream a tactile shape,
However mistily ethereal
     The half-glimpsed truth or high-flown hope.

"*Roxane* may be a daughter of Dame Nature
Or formed by wizardry of ancient knowledge
That chose from Alexander's dream each feature
     To form the blossom and the foliage.

"Many are they who make a pilgrimage
To find that Isle and gaze upon the flower;
Many they are who die for the privilege
Of being in its presence for but one hour.

"The distance is great, the perils attendant
Upon the heroic enterprise
Are fierce but serve to make resplendent
Immortal Beauty in its mortal guise.

"I am now too aged to make a trial,
Having given up my years
To meditation, toil, and self-denial,
The custom of devoted Gardeners."

Said Bear: "But your description has inspired
A strong determination to test
The power of my new-found passion. Fired
By vision of *Roxane*, I shall go in quest.

"The uproar of the stormy seas
Will not deter me, nor the tumbling snows
Of sky-peak mountains; nor will treacheries
Of villains prevent my journey to the Rose."

"Let us repair to the potting shed
And gather assorted necessaries
To aid your travel," the Gardener said.
"The better prepared, the fewer worries."

He handed him a pair of fur-lined boots,
A sewing kit, a gaily embroidered sombrero,
A microscope, two silver transverse flutes,
And further appurtenances of a Hero.

There stood Bear, knight errant without a flaw.
His mentor inspected with judicious eye,
Then gravely shook his right front paw
And bade him a cheerful, efficient goodbye.

Bear gave the Gardener a snappy salute;
He paused for a moment at the garden gate,
    Then marched off calm and resolute
    To meet his legendary fate.

The Gardener returned to the potting shed
    And entered, with smiling self-approval,
Number 40 in the ledger whose title read:
The Peaceable Gardener's Plan for Bear Removal.

An Unjust Fate

—BABRIUS

Mouse fell into
A bowl of stew
But raised no vulgar hullabaloo.
"All my life ashore I spent
On food and drink and merriment,
Devoted to pursuit of pleasure
Beyond all prudent measure.
For any Mouse who lived as I,
This is the proper way to die.
I'll gobble until I sink beneath;
Avoirdupois will bring a death
That I am sure
I can endure.
To earthly life I'll bid farewell
From my eternal home in hell."

And so Mouse swam and feasted on
Until all trace of stew was gone;
Then, from the bottom of the bowl:
"I went to heaven, after all."

The Old Woman and the Wine Jar

An old woman picked up an empty wine jar which had once
contained a rare and costly wine, and which still retained
some traces of its exquisite bouquet. She raised it to her
nose and sniffed at it again and again. "Ah," she cried, "how
delicious must have been the liquid which has left behind
so ravishing a smell."
—AESOP

Long widowed, she lived in a shack alone.
November lashed it with unmerciful rain;
December bared it to a decrepit moon;
Each day she ate two meals with a wooden spoon.

Inside her cabin, mounted upon a ledge,
A bottle stood in its place of privilege.
Before she ever was born it had been drained
Of the legendary vintage it contained.

The woman detected the original bouquet
She knew must linger there. Every day
She unstopped the crystal flask and slowly inhaled
Supernal aromas of a time unspoiled.

Through neat vineyards Pearl River made its way
Unhastily into an azure bay
Where dainty ships bobbed on the tranquil tide
And snowy egrets stood sentry side by side.

The ice-capped mountains that enclosed this nation
Handily hindered barbarian invasion,
Draping vineyards on the milder gradients
Like tablecloths in fancy restaurants.

Forests deeply interlaced with shadow;
Soft flocks grazed upon each clover meadow;
Housemaids filled their pails at the village well
And brought them home in time with the steeple knell.

The jar that contained this world was contained within
Her other world, the lonely universe
Where she lived silent, where she drank no wine,
Nostalgic for contentment that was never hers.

The Wasp and the Snake

—AESOP

Did he perceive the Snake to be
His enemy?
The Wasp, whose motive never was revealed,
Lit on the Serpent's head and stung
Repeatedly.
His victim coiled, uncoiled, recoiled
In agony,
Stabbing at the world his double tongue.

No longer willing to bear the pain, he thrust
His head beneath the wheel of a passing cart
And crushed the Wasp into the dust
And stilled his own unshriven heart.

MORAL.

They will not let us be, those episodes
We cannot unremember or deny;
They pierce like bitter knives, those words and deeds
That scar our souls until we die.

The Navigator

Anselm desires to cross the street
To a neighbor porch where a bowl of treat
He daily enjoys has been set out.
Here's the problem: It rained last night,
The forward route is shiny wet;
Icy puddles threaten his feet.

Now his inborn distaste for water
Requires that he must chart a course
Untried and perilous, to traverse
The road without a jot of spatter,
Drip, or splash, or liquidous worse.

But he misjudges and sets his paw
In a patch he thought as dry as straw
But is in fact quite the reverse.

We live in a treacherous universe.

PHILOSOPHY

Pru and Fancy

Joseph Dumasse had married Pru;
      His girlfriend was named Fantasia;
Her he treated to a holiday through
      Europe and Eurasia.

Prudence sat with the babes at home,
      Watching the fortune shrink
That once belonged to her alone.
      She began to think.

      "Never, ever trust a Dumasse,"
Pru's mother advised for the ninetieth time.
      "They're greedy and ruthless and highly low-class.
This Joe will leave you without one dime."

Her words proved prophetic. In a game of poker
      Joe dropped a million, or maybe two,
To a mildly spoken insurance broker.
      Fancy jumped ship in Sarajevo.

Homeward Joe draggled with countenance rueful,
      Mooching his way from city to city,
Ragged and hungry and not very truthful.
      "Bandits waylaid me! Brothers, take pity!"

Covered with shame and not with glory,
      At last he reached the old domicile.
To hide his behavior he concocted a story
      That Prudence greeted without a smile.

She listened ten minutes to the tale he told.
Her face grew fiery, her eyes flared amber.
"This is just more of your same old same-old."
She jacked a bullet into the chamber.

MORAL.

Imagination cannot make fools wise; but she can make them happy, to the envy of reason which can only make its friends miserable; the one covers them with glory, the other with shame.

—PASCAL

The Farmer and the Apple Tree

Farmer Nummo claimed an Apple Tree
So fruitful it sustained his family
And applejack and cider industry.

The problem was, the tree was very tall
And Farmer Nummo was of stature small,
As voluminous historians recall.

The sweetest fruit hung on the highest branches
Where Squirrels dined, sitting on their haunches.
Their eating habits made the Farmer anxious.

He named them Moochers, Slackers, Parasites,
Blamed his misfortune on their appetites
And called upon their kind a horde of blights.

Pondering how to find a remedy
To solve his problem with alacrity,
He undertook to abbreviate the Tree.

Down it came. The apples were ready to hand;
The Squirrels departed in a sullen band
From Farmer Nummo's realm of blind command.

Now he was master of his destiny,
Of his flat, unverminated property,
Of his fruitless, self-appointed royalty.

When the savages of Louisiana want fruit, they cut down the tree and gather the fruit.
There you have despotic government.
      —MONTESQUIEU, *The Spirit of the Laws*, Part 1, Chapter 13.

Of Experience

"We're off, Old Battler, for a thrilling chase
　　　　Of the notorious Hare.
　　　　Eight times before
　　　　She has eluded us
　　　　And vanished from our sight.
　　　Today that cannot be the case;
We will outrun the Rabbit they call Duchess
And bear her home before the fall of night."

　　　"And who, may I inquire, might you be?"
　　　　Replied the aged Greyhound.
"I've heard such boast from many a braggart booby
　　　　And recognize the sound.
Your prediction I do not reject,
But things may not turn out as you expect."

"They call me Rocket!" said the skinny one.
　　　"And these, my comrades in pursuit,
Are Flash and Swifty, Speed-o'-Light and Zoot.
The five of us can outrace anyone."

　　　"And yet it seems your habit
To find your homeward way without the Rabbit.
According to the nature of the hunt,
Sometimes we bring 'em back, sometimes we don't.
　　　I might put up a modest stake,
　　　Counting on a lucky break."

　　　"A friendly wager might be fun,
But what event would we be gambling on?"

　　　"I was a noted hunter once
　　　　Upon a time;

Acquired my share of local fame.
These days I rarely get a chance
              To show the skill
              That is mine still."

        "You're on!" said Rocket.
        "The wager you suggest
Is opportunity to line my pocket.
        But do you publicly declare
        That you alone will catch the Hare
        Retreating at her speediest?"

        "Indeed I do—and will put up
A dapper leash I sported as a Pup,
Also an antique silver trophy cup.
           What do you five offer
           That will bloat my coffer?"

        They haggled then about a prize
        That might find favor in his eyes.
Battler counted it a point of pride
        To seize a bargain's winning side.
        And when the back-and-forth was done
        The younger Hounds prepared to run.

        "Tally-ho!" they cried. "Not I," said he.
        "If you'll allow the liberty,
           I feel that I could use
           An antemeridian snooze.
Our bargaining plumb wore me out.
If you see Hare, send up a shout
           Proclaiming triumphal news."
        Then he lay down and placed his nose
Sleepily upon his outstretched paws.

"Well, so long, Battler. Don't forget—
And be prepared to pay your debt."
Clamorously away they went
To find and track the Rabbit's scent.

Old Battler closed his eyes to concentrate
And listen closely to the sounds
Of the five untutored Hounds,
Preparing for a lengthy wait.

"That first discordant wail
Means that they've struck a trail . . .
And now they're rushing over
Jackson's fields of clover . . .
After a refreshing stop
They take the path to Hazard Gap . . .
Now hear them splash beneath the bridge
That spans the creek on Tyler Ridge . . .
Sounds like Swifty took a fall
Scrambling over Bartram's wall . . .
So now the Hare knows where they are
And I must go and meet her where
She and I planned to confer."

The Greyhound rose and leisurely
Sought the private unmarked trail that led
Across the ferny glade
Through Coulter's Grove into the shade
Of a yellow poplar tree
Where Duchess waited patiently.

"Dear Battler," said the Hare,
"I have almost lost the knack
Of sprinting fifty yards or more

Then instantly doubling back
The way I came before.
I've reached a certain phase
Of life unseemly for the merry chase.
Perhaps it's time I should retire
And rock in bunny slippers by my fire."

"No-no. You've shown that you're in fine condition . . .
But here they come. *Let's assume position.*"

The juniors draggled into the scene,
Heaving urgently for breath,
Amazed to find Old Battler prone
With Duchess inert in his soft mouth.
He growled at them to fend away
Examination of his prey.

Next morning early they came to call
On Battler at his master's hall,
Bringing prizes he had won:
A smoking jacket of wine-dark satin,
The Odes of Horace in the Latin,
A pound of Oolong and a sticky bun.

An old greyhound will trust the more fatiguing part of the chase to the younger and will place himself so as to meet the hare in her doubles; nor are the conjectures which he forms on this occasion founded in anything but his observation and experience.
　　—DAVID HUME, *An Inquiry Concerning Human Understanding*, Section IX.

The Fox and the Man Counting Waves

—AESOP

The wrath of all the gods a man called down
                   Upon the surging sea,
Urging that the sea itself might drown.
This exercise in sour futility
                 Puzzled an inquisitive Fox
Who witnessed from the shade of dripping rocks.

         "I'm mystified. What dire occasion
Engenders such a squall of imprecation?
Has Fortune robbed you of your home and wife?
Does brutal Octopus pursue your life?
Have your strong sons turned traitor to the state?
Or was it something loathsome that you ate?"

            "Following a fertile notion,
I number all the waves of this wild ocean.
So tirelessly do those incoming mount,
At frequent intervals I lose my count—
               And then . . .
          I must begin again.

"I counted forty thousand forty-four
        Brisk surges pestering the shore
        Until a rowdy congregation
Of Herring Gulls destroyed my concentration.
I clean forgot the total from before."

       "I don't intend to give offense,
        But does your project make sound sense?
Why number objects that are numberless

Unless you wish to suffer vain distress?
　　Is it not a silly waste
　　Of life that passes in blind haste?"

　　"We scientists who watch the seas
　　Long to find anomalies;
　　　　To discover an exception
To rule is our most fortunate perception.
Then we may march, sleepless, pencil-weary,
Toward the formulation of a Theory
　　　　That overturns outdated laws
　　　　And gives our colleagues envious pause."

　　"Please let me try to understand:
You post yourself upon the shifting sand
　　　　To count the waves in hope of finding
That iron-bound rules are finally not binding.
Your previous knowledge stands a sturdy wall
Until a lone example brings its fall."

"You are a most discerning animal."

　　Fox recalled the sonneteers
Who in the quaint Elizabethan years
　　　　Considered it their business
　　　　To number all the numberless
　　　　　　Kisses, sighs, and tears
That lovesick Poets consented to confess—
　　　　Intricate, exhaustive lists
　　　　Of imaginary trysts.

He pondered this strange habit of humankind
　　　　To occupy the yearning mind

By computing many things that may not be—
Specters of Possibility,
Ingenious conceits of every kind—
From Oblivion to Eternity.

The principal difficulty in the mathematics is the length of inferences and compass of thought requisite to forming any conclusion.
                    —HUME, *An Inquiry Concerning Human Understanding*, VII, 1.

The Child and the Book

Child

You tell me water is a "molecule,"
Two "atoms" clinging to another one.
I do not feel these things upon my skin
          In my wading pool.

Book

Objects of nature must be understood
As being made of many things at once.
You cannot apprehend them at a glance
          With certitude.

Child

Can everything in my experience
Be broken into separate small bits,
Littler than the littlest tiny mites
          I cannot sense?

Book

These smallest bits are made of energies
That twirl and tumble, swerve and race
Through areas of empty space
          Like daft fireflies.

Child

The harder I attempt to comprehend,
The sooner I desert the world I know,
A place of sun and soil, of wind and snow,
          And not mere mind.

Book
Your complaints are immaterial.
My child, you can't know how to look
At things. Study me. I am a Book.
           I know it all.

Which has deceived you, your senses or your education?"
—PASCAL

Despot and Jester

Said the King to Rusticus:
"The Kingdom flames with civil disorders;
Fierce armies gather at our borders;
The wild and wine-dark Seven Seas
Are clotted with our enemies;
Wildfires ravage the forest lands;
The withered farms are cloaked in sands;
Ever-increasing unemployment
Prevents genteel enjoyment;
Blatant fraud and bribery
Compose our whole economy;
All the fabric of our time
Is stained with gruesome, habitual crime.

"Jester, as my Prime Minister,
What curatives can you prepare?"

"My King, you quickly must declare
The impropriety of war;
All rebel forces must be disbanded
Or severely reprimanded;
We must build a mighty Tower
Which will shrink one inch per hour
And where it sits completely flat
We shall site a Derby Hat.
We must protect our precious Moon
By baking a giant Macaroon
To reach into the atmosphere
And scare away the Bedbugs there.
These the methods I have found
To make our nation safe and sound."

"If so you claim and so predict,
Your words will stand as my edict,
And all shall fall out as you said.
Any Dissenter will lose his head."

"It is not to be wondered at, that Injustice and Absurdity should be insepara-
ble Companions."
—EDMUND BURKE, *A Vindication of Natural Society*

Of Privilege

When he tallied the final count
Of apples on his Stayman tree
The Farmer discovered the amount
Exceeded his Gala's three times three.

"I think I'd better spend my labor
Tending the Stayman's scrawny neighbor,"
The figuring Farmer mused aloud.
"I'll uproot saplings and compost the sod."

"I don't foresee a happy future
In that means of agriculture,"
The irritated Stayman said.
"I deserve the greater care
Because already I produce more
And stand as the more fruitful Tree.
All Nature is inequality.
If you dare dispute my right,
I will transmit a nasty blight.
Every other must bow to me."

". . . [F]or men of immoderate fortune, all power and honor not accorded
them is regarded as an affront."
—MONTESQIEU, *The Spirit of the Laws,* I, 5, 5

Lion Protector of the Hares

". . . Dear Long-Ear Friends, I think you'll find
That I deliver peace of mind.
No more will you be preyed upon
By Jackal, Puma, or Python;
No longer will the Jaguar
Devour you as nocturnal fare;
The Wolf who loves to kill by night
Will cower at home in mortal fright;
Fox will depart your lush domain
After suffering intolerable pain;
Since he deserves no nobler fate,
Polecat I will eradicate.

"So, thank you for your rousing cheers;
I've always loved my friends the Hares;
And I shall labor without surcease
So that your numbers will increase.

"How may I best aid your increase?

"I'm anxious that your tribe increase."

This is to think that Men are so foolish that they take care to avoid what
Mischiefs may be done to them by *Pole-Cats*, or *Foxes*, but are content, nay think it
Safety, to be devoured by *Lions*.
—JOHN LOCKE, *The Second Treatise of Government*, VII, 93

Creature

"Feed me," the Creature ordered. "Build my house.
Procure a fertile mate. Make up my bed.
Nourish my son and his offspring the same.
Failure of your duty brooks no excuse.
Raise my monument when I am dead
To honor me with everlasting fame."

"I will obey, if you can tell my name."

> *Man is a creature that obeys a creature that wants.*
> —MONTESQUIEU, *The Spirit of the Laws*, I, 10

Ground Level

"Whoa up, Bishop!" Immanuel Kant
Reined his plowhorse in mid-furrow.
"This earth will still be here tomorrow,
If we may trust experience,
Cleansed of all the speculative taint
That fouls the truth of physical sense.

"We'll rest us here in the breezy shade
Of this prideful Transcendental Tower.
Watch on those parapets parade
Many a brooding Philosopher,
Pondering if unsullied Truth,
Explanation bright and pure,
Can issue from a human mouth.
Their heavy robes flap all about them;
Cool winds swoop the edifice.
Contemptuous of all who doubt them,
Artifice on artifice
They mount, as they dizzily ascend
Above the region of our kind
To a mystic Ideal Cloud
Where no plowmen are allowed.

"Well, let's move on. Giddap, old Horse!
We'll act as if the dirt we plow
Is real. The other mode is worse,
To claim we can't know what we know.
Strange, how the breezes at this spot

Do not refresh. The vagrant winds
That swirl those Metaphysical minds
Do not alleviate the heat.

"We'll finish here, then find a drink.
Our world is realer than they think."

"High towers, and metaphysically-great men resembling them, round both of which there is commonly much wind, are not for me. My place is the fruitful *bathos*, the bottom-land of experience...."

—KANT, *Prolegomena*, Appendix, n. 1.

Image

Six battered decades from the babbling foyer,
Down the classroom building corridor
Dark as the focal length of the telescope
        That situates you where
      Your locker #306 awaits—
Awaited, with its scratched, familiar door
Now unfamiliar in its coffin shape—
        To divulge those secrets one forgets
        By force of effort: such as the face
        Whose memory has drawn you here.
          Or to some other place.

"So that *Imagination* and *Memory,* are but one thing, which for divers considerations hath divers names."
      —THOMAS HOBBES, *Leviathan,* Part I, Chap. 2.

FOLKTALE

The Man Who Buried His Treasure

—LA FONTAINE, X, 4

1.

"Help me find a place to hide my gold,"
      The Miser said to his wastrel friend.
      "As years plod on and I grow old,
My cash will mollify my mortal end."

"Oh, what a fortunate coincidence,"
      The man some called Two-Face replied.
      "Only yesterday I spied
An empty foxhole beside a split-rail fence.

"It runs across an unclaimed property
      In Blunder Cove, a place I doubt
      That many people know about,
Swathed in sleepy fog and mystery."

The wealthy man agreed, so they set off
      With horse and cart and money pot
      And when they reached a certain spot
Drilled cozy holes down through the duff.

There they deposited the Miser's trove,
      Taking special care to erase
      All sign of digging in that place.
Noting landmarks, back to town they drove.

2.

Alas the Miser fell in love and spent
      Great gobs of cash upon a lady
      Who was of character unsteady.
He lost his knack for canny management.

Expenses mounted. He thought what might befall
    If he refused promptly to pay
    Jeweler and couturier,
And so resorted to his principal.

But at the site he received a nasty shock.
    Spading up the hallowed ground,
    He discovered only sand,
Roots and gravel, red clay and flint rock.

Immediately he improvised a plan
    To avoid the awkward complication
    Of an unfriendly confrontation
Leading to the slaughter of a man.

3.
"Another fortunate coincidence!"
    Miser hailed Two-Face in the street:
    "I hoped that you and I would meet;
Something occurred that makes a difference.

"My uncle Rockebilt died suddenly.
    A man of lucrative affairs,
    He left behind no bloodline heirs;
His total fortune now belongs to me.

"When my schedule allows an easy day
    I shall revisit the place I keep
    My gold and add bags to the heap.
You needn't come, for now I know the way."

"To lose an uncle must be quite unpleasant.
    I tender my genuine sympathies;
    We orphans are spared anxieties
Like those that you experience at present.

"Even so, your spirit must be lightened
      With knowledge of your uncle's will
      That so increased your secret pile.
If I were you, I'd be a little frightened."

"Oh, I shall take precautions. I feel the gaze
      Of envious friends and enemies
      Who spy on my activities.
I will not view my cache for several days."

4.

Two nights later Miser was at the site,
      Rearranging the flinty soil
      With sweaty, unaccustomed toil,
Unearthing his treasure in the sly moonlight.

It was complete, to the final moidore.
      Two-Face had restored the loot
      With a dozen piddling coins to boot,
Not quite recalling the total from before.

Miser bewailed lost opportunity.
      "If only I had told Two-Face
      That I had added to the base,
He'd reimburse more than he took from me."

MORAL.

In this our time we rarely see
A Miser living in misery,
And more unlikely to see a Thief
Bound by Justice and brought to grief:
Miser and Thief develop their skills
By hot pursuit of each other's spoils.

Paddock

—GRIMM, "TALES OF THE PADDOCK"

Native to Scotland, a peculiar kind of Toad
     Locally called a *Paddock* takes
          An inordinate secret pride
     In a trove of private vanities
     Collected for their aesthetic sakes
          And hidden from envious eyes.

Scholars debate why a single breed of Frog
Developed affection for the beautiful.
A Magpie finds junk glitter suitable;
The whole idea is lost upon the Dog.

Obeying oral tradition, a wee lass laid
     The blue silk handkerchief she made,
     While spinning by the city wall,
     Outside the Paddock's residence hole.
          The sly young lassie knew
Of the Paddock's passion for the color blue.
Soon the Toad emerged with a tiny crown
     Of delicate golden filigree
     And set the splendid ornament down
     On the handkerchief for the girl to see.
     It was pleased with the display.

     But then, to its profound dismay,
     She snatched the crown and ran away.

For Toad a treasure was simply to admire,
          To hold and not to own,
Not a thing to put a price upon—
     To appreciate, not to acquire.

Its overwhelming black despair
Was such that it determined to end its life,
Unable to endure
An artless future of barren grief.
It beat its head against the wall of stone
That circumscribed the greedy town
And perished with an operatic moan.

MORAL.

Some there are for whom the beautiful
Is all in all;
Their lives require no other rationale.

The Willful Child

—GRIMM'S FAIRY TALES

"To spoil the children, spare the rod":
Falsely attributed to God,
This proverb was honored in days of yore
                 As sacred lore.

The child who was obedient
Smoothly to Paradise was sent,
If mournful circumstance applied
                 And the wee one died.

In cases where the child was willful,
Sullen, stubborn, smartass, baleful,
A different story would unfold
                 And be retold:

One small girl, whose tyrant mother
Could not control her, was a bother
Of the most vexatious kind
                 To soul and mind.

When she was twelve a raging fever
Took away this girl forever;
But, lying dead, she raised her arm.
                 Cause for alarm!

To the graveyard then they hurried;
There the child was quickly buried;
They shoveled dirt and tamped it flat
                 And that was that.

Or so they thought. From her repose
Within the ground her arm arose,
Her wrist and hand and, *cause for anger,*
     Her middle finger.

The mother grasped her birchen rod;
Down the road she swiftly trod;
At the grave she sharply caned
     That impudent hand.

When the hand withdrew from mortal sight,
It infected the rod with a birchen blight.
The mother shuddered and recoiled,
Fearing *the rod the child had spoiled*
     With all her might.

Birds and Priest

Julianna Wren

       Good morning, sister.
                     Shall we hasten,
      As the accustomed hour draws near,
      To gather with our friends to listen
      To the skinny Priest in the village square,
      To the jumbled monologue he utters,
      The grumbled phrases he softly mutters,
      The abrupt staccato he fitfully sputters,
      As he disturbs the placid air?

Julietta Wren

       Good morning, sister.
                     Let us be fair.
          We wrens should not expect
      The songs of groundlings to reflect
      Tones of feeling they may not share
          With our avian kind.
      When God created harmony
      He may have thought it a vanity
      For species of inferior mind.
      So refined an instrument
      Will not be widely prevalent.
      One thoughtful Owl has made a case
      That Birds were named the Chosen Race;
      She says we heralded the morn
              The world was born.

Julianna

      But we may not take credit for
      The gifts conferred by our Creator:
      Graceful, multipurpose wings,

Inexhaustible joy that sings
From the dawning to the latest hour,
Tuneful to the limits of our power.
If we were fated to emit such sounds
With which this fellow so abounds,
We might possess the common sense
To take a solemn vow of silence.

Maybe the noises he produces
Seem to him strains of the Muses;
Perhaps his ceaseless, bumbling Latin
Seems as smooth to him as satin.
What if that growling register
Is his sublimest vocal character?

Julietta

Or it may be that musical taste
In him would be an utter waste.

Julianna

Let us not imitate the Peacock's vice
Of Pride, lest we imitate his voice.
If we peck up the seeds he flings,
We should forgive the way he sings.
With attentive listening we do our bit,
Unlike the shameful hypocrite
Who gluttons at the hostess's table
Then slanders her with lurid babble.
This friendly Priest we cannot blame
Because our cultures are not the same.
Faulty training may be the cause
He sounds as hoarse as coarse Jackdaws.

He is a Priest,
Ordained, and tutored in the Scripture;
His mind the Holy Spirit kissed,
His soul uplifted by the rhapsodist
Who memorized King David's psalms
And set them to his harp as through the palms
He strolled in melodious rapture.
His canticle is a music other
Than ours, his temperament a different weather.
If you and I are not beguiled
By the Brother's measures shaggy and wild,
Perhaps we have been spoiled
By the happy, dulcet tone
That is our own.

We should be gracious, lest we go
To the place of carping Critics down below,
There eternally condemned to hear
Disharmonies that scorch the ear.
Let us re-educate
Our taste, as we attempt to appreciate.

Julietta
Very well, sister—if you will have it so.

Addendum.

Here is but one of the outlandish fancies
Clinging to the figure of St. Francis,
As mild and gentle as many another
About the man who called the Sun his Brother.
In further Fables stand speechifying Trees,
Forgetful Elephants, mellifluous Bees,
Animals gathering at the break of day
To hear what Francis had to say.
Not all the stories need be true,
Only the enlightening few.
Legend gathers facts within its powers
Like a Caterer selecting flowers.

The Story of Saint Felix

A clever Cat attained such grand success
    The newly invented printing press
    In chronicles and poetry
    Acclaimed his name incessantly
And so his mousing total grew ever less.

    "What good is fame? I'm too well known.
    In the farmlands and in town.
        The Mice can recognize
My whiskers and my tail, my paws and eyes,
        The lanes I prowl,
        My ominous growl:
I've lost the advantage of surprise."

        So he applied
To a scapegrace Friar who supplied
Implements of his dubious trade:
A raggedy robe with cavernous hood
Secured with a rope of foul rawhide
And sandals so worn he was nigh unshod.

"Now you can lurk to your heart's content
About those precincts where Mice haunt."

For half a season this strategy
Stocked his larger comfortably;
None saw through his quaint disguise,
Even when he was lost in thought
And from his robe his tail twitched out
And he voiced a few unconscious meows.

Then misfortune befell again:
His income slipped into deep decline.

The Mice had learned to look out for
The one they called the Devil's Friar.

"Time for me to begin anew.
The world is filled with personalities
       To serve as plausible disguise
              For a crafty hunter with stew
                     In view."

       He apprenticed to a Mummers troupe,
       Training to increase his scope
              Of methods to deceive,
       Causing victims to believe,
By means of hymn and pious platitude
       That nothing about him was Cattitude.

       To earn his keep he spent his days
       Performing in the mystery plays,
       Leaning on a shepherd's crook
       To give the manger an awestruck look,
       Impersonating Balthasar
       Who followed the magisterial Star;
       And when the Epilogue was done
       He passed the hat to everyone.

       Each time he undertook the role
Of Shepherd or Saint or figure from Allegory
That character began to shape his soul;
       The Cat was woven into the story
So closely that the holy narrative
       Determined the way that he must live.

Long nights he spent in solemn contemplation
Of scripture, striving strongly to divine

How water may transform to wine.
How wine will transubstantiate
To blood perplexed the aspiring Cat
Despite his labored interpretation.

The will of God, my brothers, works in ways
We shall not comprehend in mortal days;
The spirit of His Spirit through the ages
Abides within the Holy Gospel pages
To seize upon the thoughtful one who reads
The words of Christ and of his blessèd deeds.

Our Cat abandoned his gourmand path
And to assuage the vigilant wrath
Of God betook him to a lonely wood
And labored wholly to be good.
There he grew thin,
Embracing a rigorous regimen
Of mortification, prayer, and fasting
As he prepared for life everlasting.

He pursued these dutiful practices for
Thirteen faithful years and more.

Then on the morn of a snowy Christmas day
He died and went to heaven straightaway.
Before the Cardinals coud raise complaint
The Holy Father proclaimed him Saint,
Advising chapel altars to affix
Marble cruciform chopsticks,
As symbol of Saint Felix, who renounced Mice
To live on rice.

Scribal Addendum

As author, I rejected suppositional
    Detail and incident
    In recording this account,
  Adhering to the traditional
Story of the Saint as best we know it
      From olden Chronicler and Poet.

I am Scuttle, a humble monastery
        Mouse,
    The Scribe and Secretary
   Of l'Abbe Maistre who enjoined me
To recall the ancient legend from obscurity
        Because
He plans to revolutionize the diet
      Of the Feline population
   By means of doctrinal persuasion.
        Cats may not care for rice,
    But many are we Mice
  Who pray unceasingly they'll try it.

King and Pirate

—GESTA ROMANORUM, CXLVI

At last they chained Morbruzzo and brought him straight
To the judgment seat of Alexander the Great.

        "Are these things true
        They say of you?
    That for twenty years and more
    You looted the seas from shore to shore,
    Seizing expensive, luxurious booty
    As if the job were a religious duty,
    Cropping the ears of honest seamen
    And being unpleasant to their women?
    Murder and arson they lay at your door
    And the scuttling of the *Pinafore*.
    Pirate, you are unpopular.
    Before I pronounce my just sentence,
    Who will speak in your defense?"

"Great King, so weighty are these accusations,
I call upon the ruler of all nations
    To bring to bear his intellect
    Upon my cause. He must protect
    The principles of equal law
    Without bias and without flaw."

"Who is the spokesman you have chosen
To preserve you from death or lifelong prison?"

    "I call upon the son
    Of Philip of Macedon,
    Who read the writing of every sage
    Under Aristotle's tutelage,
    Who conquered the Thebans and enslaved

Them for the way they misbehaved,
And showed the Phrygians what was what
When he severed the Gordian knot,
And after became immensely famous,
Not for the taking of Persepolis
But for the orgy of celebration
Which for excessive inebriation
Far surpassed every festival
Of Faunus, every bacchanal—"

"Enough! It makes no sense
For me to speak in your defense.
I myself have appointed me
Your prosecutor for piracy
And crimes attendant thereunto.
I shall reveal for all to see
That you are villainous through and through
And demonstrate how from the shadows
You populate the world with widows;
I shall relate how by your word
Innocent children are put to sword.
When I have finished my haranguing,
You'll condemn yourself to hanging."

"To burn, to plunder, and to kill,
And every other piratical skill
Must be acquired, talents not given
At one's birth by grace of heaven.
You I sought to emulate;
I studied closely Alexander the Great.
Sound the bugle, strike the drum!
Morbruzzo dreams of Imperium!
In devastation and disaster
He equals the triumphs of his master.

A scurvy pirate once he was;
Now he shall make the wars and laws.
I cast my presence over every land
From Magna Graecia to Samarkand!"

"Your oration is rather curious.
Are you resolved to make me furious
By claiming I set the bad example
That led you along the path of evil?
Your wits are sharp, your mind is nimble,
Reliable assets of the Devil.
Before you draw another breath,
Know that I condemn you to death.
Did you think I'd stand still for
An equally murderous competitor?"

"No, great King, I expected
That my petition would be rejected.
I only wanted the satisfaction
Of being the object of personal action.
I can maintain with perfect candor
I'm honored with death by Alexander.
I had not reckoned my piracy
Would be written down in history.
What now the annalists will record
Stands as Morbruzzo's best reward."

"But you won't live to read the tale.
Bloody Morbruzzo, hail and farewell.
To justify each gruesome deed
You must descend from royal blood.
Your crimes would then be Victories
Over the kingdom's enemies;
Schoolboys would memorize the names
Of cities you sent up in flames
And see no reason mothers should mourn.
Better luck, Morbruzzo, next time you're born."

The Three Cocks

—*GESTA ROMANORUM*, LXVIII

First Cock

Coco-coco-cockadoo!
    Cocka-locka-cock-a-cockadoo!

Lady Ermeline

Mariette, as everyone knows,
Heaven granted you the power
To comprehend the speech of Crows,
Of Roosters, Magpies, and Jackdaws.
Pray tell me what in this sleepy hour
That trumpet Cock in the barnyard says.

Chambermaid

Milady, this Rooster is very rude,
Always in ungracious mood.
Whatever he says will bode no good.

Lady Ermeline

Mariette, your present task
Is to comply with what I ask.

Chambermaid

    "You should be true!
    You should be true!
That man in your bed brings shame on you!"

Lady Ermeline

Does he speak of my handsome gallant,
Bold Sir Perceval Malevant?

Chambermaid

I cannot fathom the thoughts of birds;
I only change their songs to words.

Lady Ermeline

If I disport with Perceval
While my spouse fights far away,
No Bird has license to tell the tale
To all the world at break of day.
Order the Cook to seize this Cock
And lay his head on the chopping block,
And let the Chronicler record
That this is the Gossip's just reward.

Second Cock

Cockalirra cockadoo
       Cockadillo dooley doo!
              Coco-coco-cock-a-doo!

Lady Ermeline

Another Rooster disturbs our peace?
Tell me, Mariette, what he says.

Chambermaid

       "You should be true!
       You should be true!
Sir Malevant brings shame on you!"

Lady Ermeline

Raised at large or in a barn,
These Roosters must be slow to learn.
Did the word not get about

Of tattling Chanticleer's headless fate?
Tell the Cook to settle this matter
By serving Bugler upon a platter.

Third Cock

Cockeldy-cockeldy-cockeldy doo!
    Cock-a-cock-a-cock-a-too!
        Crocketa-crocketa-crocketa-croo!

Lady Ermeline

What new message does this Cock bear?
I most eagerly wait to hear.

Chambermaid

"I signal for the sun to shine
Upon my Lady Ermeline,
So that all the world can view
How she is lovely, kind, and true,
How wise and faithful, and what is more,
How sweetly she treats each visitor.
Other women are called divine,
But none is saintly as Ermeline!"

Lady Ermeline

Here is a Cock deserving of fame.
Feed him whatever he may want.
Tell me, Mariette, what is his name?

Chambermaid

He calls himself Great Tantamount;
Others call him Sycophant;
Not the brightest or the strongest,
But of our Cocks he's lived the longest.

Spider and Turtle

—ASHANTI FOLKTALE

When Spider sat to eat he said a blessing,
Laid out green salad with a garlic dressing,
Anticipating roasted duck and boar;
Then heard a ponderous knock upon his door.

And here was Turtle, looking glum and poor,
Shabbier than Spider had seen him before.
He peered inside, as if he were processing
If prospects would turn cheerful or depressing.

The customs of society declare
That with the hungry traveler we share
Whatever edibles are on the table
And ample Côtes du Rhône, if we are able.

These customs Spider would not violate.
He set before his guest a stoneware plate
And said, "My friend, before you start to dine
Perhaps you'd care to wash your body clean.

"Beside the woodland path there flows a brook;
That lucent water brightens the way you look
And feel and may augment your appetite
For smoky pork rolled slowly on a spit.

"When you return I shall fill up your plate
With a cornucopia of treats to eat;
You will agree that I'm not the average cook
After you sample my honey-roasted duck."

Turtle sped along as best he could,
Oblivious to the marvels of the wood,
The glades of buttercups and fiddleheads
And cozy forms where rabbits made their beds.

In Tingling Creek Turtle immersed his shell
And all his other dusty parts as well,
Then hurried back along the toilsome path,
Undoing the effects of his cool bath.

When he arrived the spider spun a tale
Of how he fought eight thieves to no avail,
How they had taken all the food he made,
The roasted duck and boar and sweet cornbread.

Turtle, slow of foot but not of mind,
Understood what Spider had designed,
But held his peace, thinking how he might
Pay Spider back in kind another night.

And so it happened: Spider, forced to roam
Because of flooding, found the Turtle home
And, though he felt like forty kinds of fool,
Inquired of food to eat and wine to swill.

"Come sit you down!" cried Turtle. "Since last we parted
I studied sacred books and have converted
To a healthy diet." "Vegetarian?"
"I call my new style *oxygenarian*."

"*Oxy* . . . what?" "These days I live on air,
The breeze my only foodstuff, served with flair.
Tonight we sup on meadow atmosphere,
Refreshing, wholesome, and completely pure,

"So delicate it hardly weights the spoon
Transporting it from my Chinese tureen.
This zephyr was envialed when the moon
Misted midnight with its silver sheen.

"For our dessert tonight may I propose
A waft of perfume from the darling rose
Adoring plants-men name Princesse Helene
For its persuasive scent and modest mien?"

"Is this your Turtle hospitality?
I offered, when you came to visit me,
Good hearty food, the stoutest I could cook,
Pork barbecue and honey-roasted duck."

"And you may comprehend with one swift glance
That I've set out identical sustenance,
For time has not allowed me to forget
That I digested air last time we met.

"At your fine table I acquired a taste
For nothingness, ethereal and chaste.
I saw your approach and to myself I said,
'I'll feed friend Spider just as I was fed.'"

Of a Fisherman

—HERODOTUS, I, 141

An eccentric Fisherman learned to play the harp,
The cello, trumpet, and the flageolet,
Instruments of his grand strategy
To harvest flounder, tarpon, tench, and carp.

Thus he reasoned: "Music possesses power
Sufficient to cause the wild beast and the stone
To move, as if through impulse of their own,
Obedient to the wishes of the player.

"Why should I hourly cast my net and strain,
Like any dullard Ass drawing a load
Of barnyard ordure down a dusty road,
If fish will come to my bassoon's refrain?"

He tuned his oboe in the Lydian mode
And, sitting in his boat within the bay,
Invoked great Orpheus and began to play
A saltarello of the briskest mood.

The sun arose. All Nature was a-flutter
With sweet spontaneous activities;
The sky was blue, as were the seven seas.
The water in the bay lay calm as butter.

"I played so softly that they could not hear.
Fish inhabit a denser element
That cannot transport every sound and scent,
Unlike the breezes of the open air."

The Fisherman resorted to his drums,
Rolling the snare and soundly thrashing the bass;
He thumped his tympani for a bumptious space,
With mighty roaring as when a tempest comes.

To no avail. He silenced his loud clatter
And stillness allowed the Fisherman to hear
The cries of gulls, seemingly quite near,
About the isle across the placid water.

"Orpheus must have known a thing I do
Not know. Perhaps his myth is not to be
Understood as literal verity.
I judge it wise to bid my scheme adieu."

He braced and cast his customary net
In the old accustomed manner, splash and swish,
And drew it to his dory full of fish,
Lively, colorful, and soaking wet.

Now in the boat the fish began to dance,
Flopping and flapping their iridescent tails,
Flicking and flashing their iridescent scales,
Sporting, cavorting every way at once.

"I ceased performing. Why do you frolic so?
Dancing without music is a habit
Of poor, unlucky victims of the gibbet,
Who must sashay a lonely, grim solo.

"Warmth of imagination misled me
Into belief my virtuoso zither
Would draw unnumbered schools of fishes hither
As to an Oceanic Symphony."

In mute perplexity he set to work,
Grasping each and chopping off its head,
Whether it contorted or lay dead,
Laboring at his job till well past dark.

MORAL.

Inventive innovation may not improve
The ways we work for money or for love.
Sometimes retreating to the tried and true
Is the productive, prudent thing to do.

Pique

Manabozho strolled among the tents,
    Pleased with all that he had done
        Since the morning Sun
Hoisted its gold into the blue expanse.

"Last evening with the aid of lizard gizzard
    I cured a young girl's whooping cough
        And drove bad spirits off
Our burial ground. I am a powerful Wizard.

"With juices from a green sequoia leaf
    I kept at bay a deadly plague,
        Restored a severed leg,
And brought our ancient enemy to grief.

"Their hostile numbers I reduced to two;
    I formed a stallion out of sand
        Merely by waving my hand.
Is there anything I cannot do?"

These latter words a mother heard him say;
    She instantly proposed a dare
        And brought the Wizard where
On a deerskin blanket her sleeping infant lay.

It curled contentedly, with its left foot
    Happily suckled in its mouth.
        "To some she looks uncouth,"
The mother said, "but can you follow suit?"

Manabozho dropped upon the ground
    And twisted thrashing side to side.
       No matter how he tried
He could not bring his either foot around.

He rose and stalked away. He did not find
    Sufficient jealousy to change
       The babe into a being strange
And dreadful ugly. But it crossed his mind.

The Hare Who Was Married

—NORWEGIAN FOLK TALES,

PETER CHRISTEN ASBJORNSEN AND JORGEN MOE

"I've never seen you so pleased before,"
Said the curious Fox to the jubilant Hare.
"You leap and hop and bound about
And now and then you spout a shout.
What motive have you for such uproar?"

"I seize the day to celebrate.
On Maundy Thursday three weeks ago
I joined in wedlock to an eager mate
When Padre Ursus tied the knot.
I can't help grinning from head to toe."

"I had not heard your nuptial news.
Congratulations on your new wife!
She will become your light o' life,
A certain cure for lonesome blues.
I hope to meet your Better Half."

"You may have found her none so charming.
She could display an attitude
Better suited to frozen Cod,
A public demeanor truly alarming.
The dowry she brought was a cozy house
That board for board was worth her price."

"So now, Friend Hare, you own a home;
You never have to bed at night
On frosty gravel or mouldy loam
But snooze in comfort dry and tight."

"Yet I no longer inhabit there.
It fell to ash when it caught fire."

"If this catastrophe took place,
The gleeful smile upon your face
Is not consonant with the case."

"The flames that burned that edifice
Incinerated my darling spouse."

FABULISTS

Moralist and Fabulist

Moralist

Greetings, famous Fabulist!
I offer gladly to assist
Your art with polished diction and sage content.
Gentlefolk have found your tale of Horse
And randy Camel low and coarse;
It will not fetch a sinner to repent.
Also, your fable of Lady Ermeline
And of the Roosters three
Is rather naughty,
Does not conduce to piety
And some there are who think it bawdy.

I could name three dozen more
Or, at the very least, a score
Of Aesop's fables where a faithful reading
Must embarrass persons of good breeding;
But with a gentle touch
Of my Theology
I can remove all smutch
And render scandal-free,
Completely harmless for young and old,
Any fable you have told.

I can elevate a stone
To a significance unknown
By finding it a Sign
Of the heavenly Design.

An ordinary warty Toad
Becomes an immanence of God
Once I have embellished it
With allusion to Holy Writ.

Look upon that old Wheelbarrow:
Do you perceive a pulsing aura
That enfolds it like a mist
When I liken it to Christ?

I furnish your fables reverent meaning
To alleviate their vulgar leaning.

Aesop

My listeners can't sit all day;
They toil their lives away.
   His wife assists the Baker,
   The Farmer plows his acre,
The Carter whips along his cart,
The Priest entreats the Miser's heart;
They all must labor, come what may.

I speak to them of figures they well know:
The Ass and Eagle, Spaniel and pert Crow,
And if I introduce Princess or King,
They're well aware it's mere imagining.
   Sometimes I mention Elephants,
   Which I have never seen,
To add some bright variety
   To my familiar scene
With its emblematic society
Of animals without elegance.

My tales are brief and to the point,
And if a prudish Nose gets out of joint
           I think we can suppose
My point has pierced the Owner of the Nose.
      My anecdotes need no addenda
To fortify some Moralist's agenda
           Because when all is said and done,
           Fables are truly just for fun.
                 To load a solemn sermon
Upon my tale of Fox and Ermine
Is to perch a papal throne
Upon a chocolate Ice Cream Cone.

      My Fox sounds never so unwise
As when he undertakes to moralize.

The Two Bald Men

—PHAEDRUS, V, 6

Two bald men found a comb of bone
        Lying in the road.
Each one claimed it as his alone
And would knock the other's head
        With a stubborn stone.

But with debate cool common sense
Forestalled raw acts of violence
        And they applied
To great sage Aesop to decide
If justice stood on either side.

"Your impasse needs grave ponderment,"
He said. "Meanwhile appears another
Riddle, a source of tedious bother.
Yonder on that roof of thatch
A Stork awaits her egg to hatch;
Like yourselves the egg is bald,
And days are short and growing cold.
Visit Perucca's establishment
To find a wig to swaddle the egg,
Allowing the Stork to stretch her leg."
They looked at him in wonderment
Before departing on their quest
To find a wig, the curliest,
        And line the drafty nest.

"Have you concluded the task assigned?"

"Great Sage, the Mother Stork declined
With angry flapping of her wing
        Our friendly offering."

"If she rejected the compliment,
Regard the figure you present:
Two bald men have fetched a wig
      To insulate an egg,
So one of them might carry home
      A perfectly useless comb.
The reason you aroused her anger?
She thought you crazy, a probable danger;
The hapless Fool and the Lunatic
Will cause a Mother to become splenetic.
Hear my sentence, just and fair:
The comb is his who owns a Hare."

MORAL.

*The fable concerning this silly quarrel
Is better told without a moral.*

The Dog Giving Up His Prey

—LA FONTAINE, VI, 17

La Fontaine

> In this our world we fools deceive
> Ourselves from dewy dawn to eve,
> Embracing tales of miracles,
> Consulting turbaned oracles;
> There is no falsehood we will not believe.
>
> Let's keep in mind the vivid example
> Of the Dog in Aesop's fable
> Who found himself unable
> To know the Weasel in his maw
> From the other one he saw
> Reflected on the surface of a river.
> His intelligence was ample;
> In fact, the Dog was rather clever,
> But not when Nature exercised her law.
> Suddenly and totally enraptured,
> He dropped the Weasel he had captured
> To attack the image the slow water bore.
> Fifty yards downstream
> He realized that the two were not the same,
> Deceived again as he had been before.

Aesop

> You Moralists will often simplify
> The fables I originated,
> Regarding them as unsophisticated,
> Dull relics of an age gone by.

Beneath the Weasel likeness on the stream
     The Water Spaniel caught the gleam
     Of food more elegant by far.
     He plunged for a refreshing swim,
       Then paddled to the shore,
With a pearly cache of Brook Trout caviar.

Moralists perceive as mere deception
     What sometimes is the Rare Exception.

The Ape

—LA FONTAINE, XII, 19

"Beneath a mansard in Paree
Lived a brutal Chimpanzee
Who so mistreated his young wife
She lived in fear for her very life."

So begins a fable of La Fontaine.
      It seems a promising start
For a homily that all could take to heart
      And recall again and again.
      But the Poet veered aside
      From the theme he had implied
      To draw a crude
      And selfish similitude.

"Worse than he who beats the Mother
Of his Children is that other
Blackguard, the arrant Plagiarist."

We Poets are a footling race
If we believe that filching a rival's phrase
      Can injure like an angry fist.
To purloin similes may be unfair
But leaves no broken body on the stair.

MORAL.
Feel an urge to moralize?
Best order your priorities.

Aesop and His Illustrator

DEDICATED TO THE MEMORY OF FRITZ JANSCHKA

Artist

When I recall your Fable of Fox and Bust
    I see Reynard as a wary skeptic,
    His judgment marked by wry mistrust,
    Of temperament cool, of humor dyspeptic.
He examines each subject through haughty pince-nez
    Before he judges Yea or Nay,
        And when more doubtful yet,
Employs a hypercritical lorgnette.

    Is this the Reynard whom everyone knows?

Aesop

    I have seen him in that pose.

Artist

    Did he not risk communal censure
    With his awkward Turkey adventure?
        No self-respecting paragon
Of probity would tie a tutu on,
    Especially with a skirt of pink,
    Then top the ensemble with a black silk hat—
        What did the neighbors think
            Of that?

    I strive to produce a faithful portrait
    Of my subject's character:
    To paint a Magistrate's gravity,
    A Maître d's bland suavity,
    Noble features disfigured with hate:
    All these my pen shall demonstrate.

My chisel renders from the stone
The soul that is the subject's own—
But Reynard transforms before my eyes.

Aesop
I have known him in multiple guise.

Artist
With fulsome flattery he tricked the Crow
To drop her dinner into his paw,
Presenting himself as a connoisseur
Of vocal art.
I posed him as false master of a choir
In my accurate, tart
Caricature.
When during the trial of the Missing Lamb
He pled his case in court
I limned him as a lawyer suspecting sham
And eager for legal tort.
When Fox set out to learn the gist
Of Wild Boar's plan for self-defense
He played the role of journalist
With a ready tape recorder
And in short order
Gathered fruitful intelligence.

To pursue his course of arrant flummery
Fox requires a large costumery:
Capacious armoires of cedar and oak
Stocked with every style of cloak,
Masks of Bears and Wolves and Pigs,
False beards, aristocratic wigs,
Many-colored shades of talc,
Powder, rouge, greasepaint, and chalk:
All the accoutrements of disguise.

Aesop

Reynard deceives all vigilant eyes.

Artist

But my stylus must disclose
The true Reynard whose borrowed clothes
Cannot conceal the felon he is,
Whatever his varied appearances:
Sardonic smile that hints of cruelty,
Handsome pelt admired by female
Humans, an outsized tail
Curling continually,
Acutely pointed ears, a knowledgeable nose
And penetrating eye.
He steals through life with impunity,
Attentive to any opportunity
To filch from Hen-coops, Housewives, Shepherds, and Crows.

Aesop

So must we all suppose.

Artist

My task is thus twofold:
To present the Reynard the populace sees
And simultaneously the Fox he is
In his true mold.

Aesop

Now you have described the heart
And purpose of my own art.

Aesop to Fox

The Fox who frisks about my Fables
Is not the fox of zoology;
She is a Persona that enables
Your servant Aesop to display
Dilemmas of the Human Species
With figures righteous or downright vicious.
In short, my Vixen is a mask
That suits requirements of my task.

A portrait of you as you are,
A truly complex character,
Ambiguous, ambivalent,
A trickstress unmalevolent
With a particular code of honor,
Strains the limits of the genre.
My narratives enlist the power
Of the art of caricature.

The Squirrel hoards nuts. Is he a miser,
Or does he pertly personify
Some happy qualities of a wiser,
More foresightful mentality?
Not every Lion is strong and bold;
Many are ailing, blind, and old,
But the Lion of my stories
Is clothed in customary glories
So that his story may be told
By a Fabulist such as I.

From a wildwood friend I seize a trait,
Color it shiny, exaggerate
Its special peculiarity,
Place it within an anecdote
Couched in the pseudo-rustic style
So as to tease a rueful smile
From one who prefers unpolished wit
And comprehends, in afterthought:
"Why am I laughing? Vixen is *me*."

To draw an intricate personage
Requires a Chekhov or a Proust;
To perch four Turkeys on a roost
Is the method of the Fabulist
In this our golden Classical Age.
I make no claim as Novelist,
As Epic Poet or Dramatist;
My role is modest: to set the stage,
To demonstrate, and then desist.

With calculated humility
Fables retain ability
To occupy their lower station
In the Republic of Literature
While yet compelling the fascination
Of the learned connoisseur
Who concurs with their major point:
This world was fashioned out of joint.

Vixen to Aesop

In two score fables by my count
You have assailed my character,
Portraying me as fraudulent,
Untrustworthy, of mean descent,
Stealthy, underhanded, sly,
Quickly given to tell a lie—
And I resent your every slur.

We, the laborers of the night,
Accustom ourselves to social slight,
To insult, and to accusations
Intended to smudge our reputations.
Such is ever the unjust way
Of those privileged to work by day
And think themselves the grander creature
Because of an accident of nature.

The Fox who heads a family
Acquires responsibility
To shelter, instruct, and feed four kits
With truly astounding appetites.
I choose to pursue the hunt alone
Under the frosty midnight moon,
Taking the rat, the shrew, the beaver—
Every small gnawer whatsoever—
And when I'm lucky now and then
I treat my brood to a big fat hen.

You will say I'm a lawless thief,

That I should turn my life around.
If you were harried by horn and hound,
You might adopt a new belief.
The Moralist should calmly withhold
His stern indictment narrow and cold
And seek to discover what circumstance
Brought the subject to mischance.

How would Aesop contrive to thrive
Outside the household of his master?
Brother Aesop is a slave,
Meek donkey in a thorny pasture,
Bound about as in a thicket
Of iron chain and ruthless picket,
While swathed in moonlight on the hill
Wary Vixen lopes where she will.

Against the sky her silhouette
Confirms a friendly relationship
With every aspect of the night:
Blue stars drifting a powdery light
Along the watchful mountaintop,
The close breeze lisping secretly
To the languid willow tree,
The moon that in a linen shroud
Wanders spectrally abroad—
Across this landscape Vixen roams free;
Nighttime is my sanctuary.

Aesop at the Shipyard

—AESOP

It happened that sage Aesop found his way
To the sheltered inlet of a harbor bay
Where forty shipwrights labored mightily,
Building a vessel to sail the wine-dark sea.

The burliest of them mocked the aged man:
"O, Champion Idler since the world began,
Too dull to fabricate a full-blown tale,
Your Fables one could write on a horseshoe nail.

"Where are your Character Development,
Your Narrative Arc and Telling Incident,
The sweet, impassioned speech of lover to lover?
Once you begin a tale, it's well nigh over."

"I see you ready to step your mizzenmast,
A piddling thing of thirty feet at best.
Since you think good to undergo such toil,
Why not mount one that measures half a mile?

"I could skein out my pithy Fables longer,
If I considered I might make them stronger,
But I prefer to fit them with a size
Not easy to adulterate with lies."

"But time is coming when the longer story
Will bring its author fortune and bright glory.
The Shepherd and his Wife in their dank hovel
Will read by firelight something called a Novel.

"Soon your quaint vocation is no more;
The future has a different style in store.
Your days are numbered, ancient Fabulist.
Chanticleer and Reynard will not be missed."

"All was water when the world began,
All but the silent furnace of the Sun,
Until great Zeus decided to present
Existence to another element.

"He requested Mother Earth to take three swallows.
She drank. Tall mountains thrust above the billows
And cast the world's first shadows majestically
Upon the surface of the diminished sea.

"Obedient to command, she drank again.
Below the mountains spread a worldwide plain;
Horizon to horizon and beyond
Lay the pasture and the desert land.

"If thirsty Terra takes but one sip more,
She will reveal a curious ocean floor,
Supporting no ocean but the lucid air
With hummingbirds like minnows swimming there.

"You foretell the passing of the Fable.
When this whole world is flat as a marble table,
Brittle, dry as a Parian marble chip,
How shall you launch your proud three-masted ship?

"A Fable finds, alas, too soon its end;
So feel we all about our lives, my friend.
We each perform a role and then are gone,
Unlike the Novel, gabbling on and on."

Fox

Fox and Crow

Fox spots Crow in the top of a Pine.
"That tapas she savors must be mine."
He ponders how to ply his wit
And award himself the whole of it.

"Who is that who trills so grand?
The great soprano Dame Sutherland,
Whose voice charms every audience
For Sydney, Australia, to Paris, France.
O fortunate hour! What blessing is mine
To catch a glimpse of the Diva divine!
Can I persuade you, just for me,
To sing one bar of 'Un' bel di,'
Or the 'Air des bijoux' of Charles Gounod,
Or a single note of 'Dove sono'?"

Crow, unused to being wooed,
Quickly finds a musical mood.
She fills her lungs and sings *"Croaw!"*
And delivers her morsel into Fox's paw.

MORAL.

The Flatterer has a plan in mind
That many not benefit all mankind.
His words are honey, his smile is warm;
His hand in your pocket intends no harm.

Fox and Turkeys

—LA FONTAINE, XII, 18

Four Turkeys huddled in a hickory tree
       Watching the space below,
A grassy circle enclosed with hedge,
In the design of a vaudeville stage,
Where these Turkeys enjoyed to see
When a performer put on a show.

Roosting, they felt snug and secure,
Safe from harmful circumstance,
Like Wolf and Jackal, Lynx and Bear,
And though the Fox might dare the chance,
He could not scramble to their height,
          Try as he might.

This night as the pearly Moon
       Her placid countenance shone,
The Fox, according to plan, appeared
In a pink tutu and black top hat
And a bristly ginger-colored beard,
And fell expertly upon his prat.

Then, not a bit the worse for wear,
He leapt five feet into the air,
And landed on point most admirably.
Assuming a posture debonair,
He searched his tail for a comical Flea
Which would never sojourn there.

He sang, he spoke
Irreverently of Shepherds and told a joke
About a Chicken who crossed the road
Transported by a gullible Toad.
    He danced the jig
Of Ernestine the Inebriate Pig.

   It is a foul canard,
That Turkeys have no sense of humor.
These four Turkeys laughed so hard
They utterly destroyed that rumor,
And lost their purchase on the bough
And struck the sod *ker-plunk ka-pow.*

The Fox crammed them into his sack
And tied it tight with miller's twine
And slung the lot across his back
And bore them home to serve with wine.
What he uncorked I do not know,
But *I* would pour a nice Bordeaux.

MORAL.
Laugh if you will, but don't laugh your head off.

The Streamlined Fox

—AESOP

"We Foxes must not drop behind.
The times are changing fast as the wind
That swoops along the mountaintop.
Once we fall back, we won't catch up.
This brave new world is built for speed,
Discarding all it does not need:
No excess baggage, surplus fat,
Rhetorical flourish, no silk top hat.
To validate our species credentials,
We must strip down to the essentials,
Becoming lean and lithe and narrow,
As ready to purpose as the well-aimed arrow.
To ensure that Foxhood does not fail,
We must jettison the tail."

The assembly he had gathered there
Turned on Red a bewildered stare,
Trying collectively to find
If he'd completely lost his mind,
Each Fox present tried to picture
What he'd be like without the fixture
Of his lush brush and frisky tip
To curl about and flaunt and flip.

Now an elder Gray spoke out:
"You are sincere, I have no doubt,
But as you spoke I glimpsed your butt.
Nothing is there but a pitiful scut
That even a Hare would bear with shame.
Trying to understand your game,
I formed a theory. I will bet
That in the trap the Farmer set
A tail lies there, abandoned, lone,
The very tail you called your own.
I'll wager that the plan you suggest
Is the one that serves you best,
Disguising your deficiency."

"No! My concern is efficiency!
No more pointless, idle wag
No more aerodynamic drag!
You have failed to grasp my notion—"

His speech was halted by a commotion
Erupting in the rear of the hall
Where Vixens had settled one and all.
Four Kits had disobeyed their mother
To chase the tails of one another,
Reminding all of a homely truth,
They too chased tail while in their youth.

The Fox and the Cat

—GRIMM'S FAIRY TALES

This Cat was a modest being
Who greatly admired a prideful Fox.
He stored a thousand clever ways of fleeing
The Hounds filed in his brain as in a box,
He habitually claimed.
"All about the country I am famed
For sly subtility
That instantly enables me
To find out hiding places
Where Canines never show their faces . . .
How many artful dodges do you know?"

"One only," said the Cat. "To escape
A predator or foe
I nimbly leap
Into a tree
Where foliage camouflages me.
I do not move or mew a sound
To draw the notice of the Hound.
In my Hemlock I will stay
If necessary for that whole day,
Watching until the Plott is called away."

"I lead old Plott a breathless chase,
Streaking comet-like from place to place,
Then doubling back
Upon my track,
Employing every mite of hustle
To draw confusion to his muzzle.
Traipsing through the pearly flow,
Up and down the creek I go.
If sorely pressed I will slip in

To a deserted Groundhog den;
And if he catches up with me,
It's not a Fox that he will see
But a humble Monk instead
With a cowl masking his head,
Or a coy Milkmaid petite
Clopping about on sabot feet,
Or a learned Botanist
Clutching purslane in his fist.
Within the thickets, amid the trees
I have established costumeries—"

"Oh, Master Fox, please do beware!
The Hunter and his Hound are near!"

"I know where the shadows lie
That lend invisibility;
Not the keenest eye perceives
Where I crouch among the leaves,
And with the onset of the night
I lope entirely lost to sight—"

"Too late, too late! I cannot bear—
Oh! Master Reynard is no more!"

The Hunter ended his dire business;
He left the scene a bloody mess,
Never suspecting Cat was there.

Fox and Corncrib

—HORACE, *EPISTLES*, I, 7

Once there was a slender, supple Fox
Almost as skinny as a fashion model.
By moonlight you could count his every rib.
Nosing a lucky hole in a corncrib,
He slid through like a straw into a bottle
And gobbled corn like a malnourished Ox.

A Weasel who observed the episode
Wondered how the Fox could retrace his way.
"My friend, you've swollen like a bloated Toad.
Appears to me that you may have to stay
Enclosed until you slim to exit size.
So: meditation, daily exercise—
And readjust your gluttonous attitude."

"But why should I adopt a sour, ascetic
Regimen when all is copacetic
Status quo? I have here close at hand
Plenty to satisfy my appetite.
No more the anxious hunt across the land
All the howling, hound-infested night."

"Do you never long for the good old times?
The splendor of the unobstructed moon,
Breezes bearing the distant belfry chimes
At midnight, scouting the mountainside alone
By starshine—"
                    "I prefer my corncrib life.
It lacks excitement and variety
And I regret I am no longer free
To roam. But now I have security—"

"Yet here comes Farmer, sharpening a knife."

The Fox and the Horse

—THE COMPLTETE GRIMM'S FAIRY TALES

I.

"You ask why I am so dejected,"
To curious Fox the Horse replied.
"Within this hour I was rejected
By one with whom I labored side
    By side for many years.
The Farmer turned me out, despite my prayers."

"What reason could he plausibly give?"
The sympathetic Fox inquired.
"He is not able to let me live
At his expense. I am retired
    Because so elderly
That he can find no further use for me."

"Is there no way you can appeal?"
The enterprising Reynard asked.

"If there were some way to fulfill
The fearful charge that he has tasked,
    Maybe I could stay
In residence until some future day.

"But how shall I subdue a Lion?
I am no seasoned warrior
Or mighty hunter like Orion
Who once slew Lions by the score.
    'Capture that beast,' the Farmer said.
'Such heroism will keep you housed and fed.'

"This pact he offered I accepted.
There seemed to be no other choice,
But I am ancient, long decrepit,

Brokenhearted, weak of voice,
    Lacking energy."

 "Let us devise a strategy.
I will employ a ruse to aid you,
For you have plowed such faithful furrows
Your just reward must not evade you.
Let me supply your glad tomorrows
    And then in time's due course
I'll seek repayment from my friend the Horse."

II.

Sly Fox instructed Horse to lie
    Perfectly still. "Don't twitch
    An eyelid or scratch an itch.
Our scenario is that I
Discovered you beside the road
    Wholly intact but wholly dead.

"I'm going now but shall return with one
Who wears a mane as my companion.
    Your miming will prove salutary
Only if you lie here stationary."

III.

Fox accosted Lion in the wood:
"Old pal, I have discovered something good.
Let's go inspect this enticing source of food . . .

"And now you see, friend Lion, that what I said
Is true. Old Bill the Horse, supine beside
    The road he used to plod, is dead.

"Unluckily for me, last night
I ate a rancid partridge. My appetite
Has not recovered. I do not feel aright.

"So now this Horse belongs to you alone
Sumptuously to dine upon . . .
If so inclined, you might spare me a bone.

"But dusty ditch-side dining is no fun.
Let me tie him to your tail, and then
You can transport him to your den."

Exercising caution anigh the claws,
Fox lightly bound the Lion's hinder paws
With an extremely complicated truss.

He wound
Each strand
About and around
With such nice art
That every knot
And every plait
Seemed tight and snug
But would come apart
With one sharp tug.

So, Old Bill held Lion in his power,
Apparently. It was performance pure
For which they had rehearsed a solid hour.

Old Bill set out upon the byroad for
Hiram Burleigh's sturdy farmhouse door
And knocked three hearty knocks and not one more.

IV.

"What do my wondering eyes perceive?
Old Bill returned with a Lion in tow?
A phenomenon hard to believe,
Surpassing everything I know."

Farmer Burleigh stood in amaze,
Surveying the pair with astonished gaze.
"Your upkeep I shall not refuse,
But for the Lion I have no use.
I'd much prefer that he were gone.
I'll fetch my rifle and put him down."

When Burleigh marched off to his study
Horse shook his tail and Lion was free.
Old Bill whispered, "So long, buddy.
In your prayers remember me."

Fox and Bust

—LA FONTAINE, IV, 14

Observe how Fox observes his universe,
How he examines each detail with care,
    Suspecting that the way things are
    Is not the way they seem to be.
"Appearance," he says, "infrequently concurs
    With reality.

    "When they unveiled the bust
    Of our late Senator
Unmourning colleagues thundered accolades
    That glorified his dust,
    Extolling him as among the shades
Of those grand solons who came before.

"The Sculptor framed him better than he should:
    A noble forehead, a searching gaze
    That seemed acutely to pierce one's soul,
    Aquiline nose and resolute jaw.
    In that hour his cohorts said
He was a guiding spirit of our days,
    In whom inhabited the full
    True import of our law.

"When they were gone, I approached the pedestal
    To compare this carven semblance
    With that of my old acquaintance.
    Sad to relate,
The nose was taken from Alexander the Great
    As rendered by Apelles;
    Those searching eyes
    From Pericles;

The forehead belonged to Hadrian;
And Caesar's, that determined chin.
The only attribute I'd name his own—
The brain of stone.

"I wondered as I left the hall
Where similar busts lined every wall,
Were they like him, each one and all?
And so came out
Consumed with doubt,
Surmising that cool marble reveals
A great deal less than it conceals."

Fox and Grape

—AESOP

Fox reclined beneath a Vine,
    Arranging the billow
    Of his tail as pillow,
And plinged his indolent mandolin:
"O refulgent mini-Moon,
I shall clasp thee very soon.
O my golden Scuppernong,
Alluring subject of my song,
Divine raceme of my festive dream,
You shall provide me sumptuous fare
When I ascend to where you are."

A skeptic Mouse from her hiding place
Said, "Fox, my friend, that ain't the case.
Jump as high as ever you can,
You must fall short by a generous span."

Fox rippled chords, and then, at length:
"Mouse, you underestimate my strength.
I run strong with relay teams
When they compete in Olympic games;
A hurdle is no barrier
When I surmount a barnyard fence
As if the structure were not there
To become the guest of friendly Hens.
The incompetent Judges were at fault
Who barred me from the Spring pole vault
Because, they claimed, my plentiful tail
Serves as illegal aerial sail.
I will perform a prodigious leap
And gain possession of the Grape."

"I'm no gambler, but I will bet
That nothing a-plenty is all you'll get.
You may boast the whole day long,
But you won't seize the Scuppernong."

Everyone knows the end of the tale,
The more he tried, the worse he'd fail;
He'd bound and leap and blithely soar,
But not one Grape could he ever score.

So he dawdled for a thoughtful hour
And tingled on his instrument
Before declaring, "Those Grapes are sour!
There's something metaphysically wrong
With this particular Scuppernong.
It is no edible aliment.
The dreadful taste of its putrid must
Would grip my gut like an angry fist;
My mouth would never forget the feel
Of its disgusting, slimy hull;
I would require swift medical help,
If I ingested its gruesome pulp,
And if I swallowed a single seed,
My Foxhood would shrink to a rosary bead.
You'd better take my wise advice
And warn the innocent, unwary Mice:
Here hangs the deadly Grape from Hell."

Retorted Mouse, "So now we know—
What then, Reynard, will you do?"

"Inadequacy of this Grape for food
Is theme for Aesop to include
In his *Collected* when he is able
To produce a final, telling Fable.
This Vine deserves no further look;
I'll amble home and read a Book."

PARABLE

Parable of the Trees

—BOOK OF JUDGES, 9:7-15

The Trees once felt a great desire
To choose one of themselves as King.
First the Olive they petitioned,
But it refused the role envisioned:
"If I would do as you require,
Then I must cease my reverent toil
Of producing essential oil
To be as monarch a useless thing."

Then to the Fig they made request.
"No, I must do as I think best.
I shall continue to bear the fruit
That poet and minstrel chant about
When it appears in the smiling feast."

And next the Trees approached the Vine,
Asking it to assume their reign.
"The gods and mortals cherish the wine
That lifts the hearts of everyone.
Let another mount the throne;
My royal purple remains my own."

The desperate Trees thought to inquire
Of the brusque, ill-tempered Briar:
"O Pyracantha, take the scepter
We acknowledge as the symbol
Of a Monarch and Preceptor
Over us, your subjects humble."

"Well . . . Maybe we can strike a deal,
Depending on the way I feel.
Do you offer in good faith,
Or will you perjure your sworn word
In future time, and seek my death
With reaper's sickle, scythe, or sword?
I advise particular care
After the final contract is drawn.
I have in me sufficient fire
To burn the cedars of Lebanon."

The Parable of Nathan

—2 SAMUEL, 12: 1-7

"There was a wealthy man possessed of sheep,
         Of cattle, goats, and fowl;
He enjoyed feasts and luxurious sleep
         And took no care about his soul.
         He was immoderately bound
                  To material things he owned.

"Nearby there lived a poor industrious neighbor
         Obliged to him for a modest debt;
This man lived by dint of personal labor,
         Daily comforted by a pet
Ewe lamb he fed at table from his own hand,
Of which his children were extremely fond.

"Lately there arrived a Visitor
         Who traveled the thirsty countryside
         Collecting provision for the poor
         Whose number drought had multiplied.
         The wealthy man called in as forfeit
         The lamb that was his neighbor's pet
To pronounce the obligation satisfied.

"A sorrow like the smoke of dying fire
         Darkens this farmer's home;
         His children weep because the lamb
         Is lost to them forever more."

"Bring me the miscreant that took
From them their animal," King David ordered.
"I desire to look
Upon his face as he is drawn and quartered.
For that lost lambkin he must pay his life."

Thus the prophet Nathan spoke: "You sent
Uriah to his death and took his wife.
Thou art the man. Thou art that *miscreant.*"

MORAL.

Some parables point a simple meaning
And do not need explaining.

The Wheat and the Tares

—GOSPEL OF MATTHEW, 13:24-30

Attend the Sower's fable!

A thoughtful Farmer went out to sow
        His field with wheat
    So that the stalks would grow,
Supplying him with bread to eat.

His land conjoined an envious neighbor
Who sought to nullify his labor
By over-sowing the field with seeds
        Of noxious weeds.

His servants complained. "What can be done?
How shall we pluck them one by one,
        Each little sprout
Impossible to single out,
So close a likeness invaders bear
      To plants that we desire?"

Said the Farmer, "Let us spare
      Ourselves such toil and wear.
Time will distinguish what we need
      From the useless weed.
Allow the fullness of time to grow them;
By their fruits then we shall know them.
As they develop in the field together,
One will differ from the other.

"Every seedling must mature
Before we know its character;
In due season we shall learn
Which sheaves to store and which to burn."

The Leaven

He then told them another parable. "The kingdom
of heaven is like leaven which a woman hid in three
measures of meal, till it was all leavened."

—GOSPEL OF ST. MATTHEW 13:33

  ST. LUKE 13:20-21

A few there were who understood the words
Of Christ among that restive multitude:
He counseled against the taking up of swords
To darken the nation Israel with blood
Of children, wives, the blind and elderly.
The grizzled veterans of dusty wars
Noted carefully each passerby
And nursed with tankards their familiar scars.

He used the metaphor of leavening
A woman hid away in her coarse meal
To work its subtle power gradually
And multiply the volume of the whole
By fermentation observers will not see:
The strategy of Martin Luther King.

Go For It

—GOSPEL OF ST. MATTHEW, 13: 44

Shortcutting through his neighbor's stony field,
    A Farmer noticed in the scene
    A momentary golden shine
    By impure color undefiled.
Was this the moment when Dame Fortune smiled?

"A Treasure hides itself within that ground;
    Unknown for decades, it has lain
    Undisturbed by plow or rain,
    Never likely to be found
If I had hiked the other way around.

"A chest contained the gold until decay
    With its unceasing, silent toil
    Rusted the latches in the soil
    So that the leather sides gave way
And thrust a coin into the light of day.

"Then God revealed to me His clear command:
    To sell whatever belongs to me
    And buy this barren property
    Of thorns and gravel, weeds and sand,
So that the happy gold comes to my hand.

"If I can do what God Almighty says,
Then I shall live in pleasure all my days."

MORAL.
    Be he Cool or be he Square,
    God loves the Man who takes a dare.

Black Cat and Evening Star

Tabitha

> I most admire your serenity.
> You sail alone and motionless
> Within a slowly purpling sea
> As hour by hour the sun grows less.
> Your course is steadfast from eve to dawn.
> Golden and aloof you poise
> Above the world you gleam upon,
> Its endless sorrows and infrequent joys.
> Lone you are, and loneliness
> Is what you lighten and what you bless.

Hesperus

I envy your engagement with the night.
To its great darkness you give up your own.
Omnipresent in the absconded light,
You are everywhere at once till night is gone.

The world is yours to reconnoiter at will
When sun departs the unreluctant sky
And twilight smudges the steeple and the hill
And the last breeze passes with a passive sigh.

Then you join the anonymity
Of nameless shades of shadows that swarm the dark
With eyeless darknesses, a unity
Of separate beings without name or mark.

MORAL.
With Self-possession I may meet the Night
*   And guide my Self by my own Light;*
Or at the Advent of that long Nightfall
*   Give my Self over and embrace the All.*

The Boasting Lamp

BABRIUS

The night the Lamp got drunk
    On oil of Cannabis seed
He boasted when he said
    His light was brighter far
Than that of any Star,
    Brighter than every light
In the Sky's unbounded height—
    And a lot of similar bunk.

Then came a lively Breeze
    That with careless ease
Extinguished with one puff
    The braggart. She'd had enough.

MORAL.

This little light of mine,
    I shall let it shine,
But I will never claim
    It is a leaping flame,
For many times the Liar
    Invites his own despair.

The New and the Old

There was a Scribe who set down as instructed
    The words intended to be transcribed.
    He also of his own accord
    Set down many another word
    That in his memory had survived
Original, unchosen, unobstructed.

He listened carefully to the Counselor,
    Spelled out his maxims one by one,
    Correcting none, mistaking none,
    Exalting the high oracular,
    Recording the rude vernacular
Accurately, until the speech was done.

And when he came to read the discourse over,
    He found there phrases and similes
    Clustered like gleaming honey bees
    On blossoms of white pasture clover,
    Figures the Counselor had never
Spoken, wise and learned mysteries.

What a grand Vision the Counselor revealed!
    Part of it was known before,
    Stored safely in the common lore,
    By homely commoness concealed;
    Yet now it shone forth like a star
That all had long observed while unaware.

"Then said he unto them, Therefore every scribe which is instructed unto the kingdom of heaven is like unto a man that is a householder which bringeth forth out of his treasure things new and old."

—GOSPEL OF MATTHEW, 13:52

PREAMBLES

If we may posit, for purposes of organization, a class structure for the society of the dramatis personae of the fables, we will devise a system that resembles both the monarchies of the classical eras and the feudalism of the middle ages. The lines between the social classes of the fables cannot be so sharply drawn as in those historical systems. The fables were not consciously designed to depict a society; they are mostly concerned with the relationships between individual members of the classes.

Many fables recount episodes of class-conscious confrontation. These often state or imply that the social system in place is immutable and unimprovable and that it is good for any individual to acknowledge and behave in accordance with her or his place in the system.

I recall a familiar southern Appalachian proverb: "Best not try to get above your raisin's."

Herewith follows a rudimentary hierarchy built upon simple analogies. The categories will frequently overlap, as in all societies.

Divinity: The gods and goddesses

Royalty: Kings and Queens, Lions and Lionesses

Nobility: Eagles, Bulls, Cocks, Wild Boars, Ornamental Fowl, Roses

Intellectuals: Scribes, Priests, Fabulists (usually Aesop as persona), Prophets and Soothsayers, Philosophers, Songbirds, Mice, Minor Clericals

Yeomanry: Farmers, Fishermen, Hunters, Horses, Crows, Dogs and Hounds, Cats, Deer, Apes, Bears

Peasantry: Plants, Serpents, Rats, Insects, Inanimate Objects (Lamps, Pens, Jars, etc.) Sheep, Asses, Hares, Domestic Fowl, Goats, Pigs

Outliers: Children, Wolves, and the *Fox.*

The inclusion of a class of intellectuals may seem anachronistic; their denomination as a class is usually dated from the rise of the universities in the twelfth century CE. But in the fable society certain functions can be performed only by thinkers, teachers, orators and, others who are literate.

Fable society also includes plants and insects and in this regard the fabulists preceded contemporary scientists and theorists like Michael Pollan, E. O. Wilson, Michel Foucault, John Hartigan, Jr., and others who view an ecology as a society that includes microorganisms and soil types as members. The inclusion of inanimate objects as actors anticipates our daily interactions with computers and with emerging Artificial Intelligence entities.

Determinants of caste are principally two, characteristics and functions. These are not separate qualities, though they are distinguishable. The characteristics of a persona will usually assign it to certain functions. The Hound is swift, eager, and determined; therefore, he is a hunter and thus a member of the Yeomanry. The Wild Boar is an independent, self-sufficient master of a limited territory; he is an unkempt and ill-mannered Noble.

Most personae claim their social status because of their usefulness to the society as a whole; their physical and mental capacities assign them to certain roles. Prized qualities include physical strength and endurance, predatory skills, physical appearance, intelligence, cunning, foresight, fleetness, abilities to hide and to observe, wit, and self-knowledge. Possession of a few or even only one of these characteristics is sufficient to secure a place in rank. The Lion has no need of cunning nor the Bear of speed.

Some personae do not fit into these categories; they are significant outliers. Children, including the offspring of animals, seem situated in an ambiguous space; their roles are variously assigned. Wolves are individualists, loners fearful of society and sometimes contemptuous of it. They are arbitrary in their actions and often cynical in outlook.

The *Fox* is a complex personality and is given a section of this volume all his own.

SOCIAL FUNCTION

My classification of the social strata of fables is inexact, artificial, and in some respects almost arbitrary. Social *class* is not clearly distinct from social *function*. These qualities are nearly inseparable. Class may determine function; the Lion as Royalty must rule, protect, and sometimes adjudicate. Function may determine class; the Ass as Peasant or Slave must perform the heaviest labors, following the orders of social superiors who are not often kindly in his regard.

And neither of these classifications is completely separable from *psychology,* the individual mind-set of each of the personae.

Where there are Sheep there will be Shepherds; the function of the Wolf as predator makes Sheep and Shepherd dependent upon each other. If the persona cannot fulfill its socioeconomic function, it becomes an outcast, as in the case of the aged Lion and Horse. Sometimes a persona may rebel against its allotted function and become a successful innovator or an unsuccessful social climber. The Chimpanzee who learns to climb trees sets a progressive example; the Crab who deserts his beach environment for green pastures betrays his preordained place in the world and loses his life.

Within their narratives the personae of the fables resemble the cast of television situation comedies. The main player possesses a stable temperament; he or she is continually bemused, annoyed, tempted, and sometimes embarrassed, yet manages to regain equanimity in the end. The neighbors, friends, and colleagues are eccentric in some fashion: naive, ignorant of certain facts or mores, bibulous, socially awkward, odd in physical appearance, timid, overbearing, pedantic, and so forth. Their narrative functions are fixed and they fulfill them as their proper roles in life. The social function of the eccentrics is to offer contrast to the imputed norms of the pocket society of the sitcom they inhabit, the norms the main player embodies.

The central character of a sitcom is the Lion of a fable, possessing some freedom of choice, sound judgment, power to act, and desire for peacefulness. The lethargic neighbor is the Bear, the delightful ingénue is the Sparrow or Songbird, delivery men are the Asses, the self-centered advertising executive is the Peacock. This list of pairings can be extended at length.

If the use of stock characters points up the rudimentary nature of sitcoms, it also makes possible the brevity of fables because of predictability. As soon as Wolf appears, we are sure we know what is on his mind. If he is dressed as a priest, we are even more certain.

PSYCHOLOGY

The Cat knows what she is as an individual and as a member of her species and social class. She knows that her thoughts will always be Cat thoughts, but she knows too that the Boar will think Boar thoughts and the Eagle will act according to his role in the scheme. This knowledge gives her freedom to act in her own best interests because she can predict the motives and actions of those she plans to influence. If she had to act without such knowledge, she would endanger herself and her offspring.

"They will act," she thinks, "for their self-preservation—just as I do. Therefore, I can persuade them by means of fear."

In this instance, the Cat pits Reason against blind Instinct and this same conflict, Reason versus Instinct, plays out in numerous other fables. The advantage of reasoning power is attributed variously as the stories require, to Hares and Mice and Bulls.

Even Trees have enough self-consciousness to ponder their plight. Then, when a new situation arises, the fabulist confers Reason upon another persona and then the Cat may have to be dependent upon Instinct, as in "The Fox and the Cat."

Reason is not always triumphant. The reasoning Lamb is devoured by the Wolf, who in some instances may personify Instinct. Yet there are fables in which the Wolf resorts to reason only to find Instinct the more reliable principle.

In almost all cases, both reasoned and instinctive actions are motivated by self-preservation. As in actual conflict, an outcome may go either way, depending upon the moment.

PHILOSOPHY

"Philosophy," as its name asserts, is "love of wisdom." The kinds of wisdom expressed in fables may seem at a casual glance rudimentary or even raw when compared to the pages of Kant, Hegel, Popper and other sophisticated mentors. Yet beneath the complex superstructures of those systems we may often discover concise formulations that resemble the appended Morals of Fables. In the books of the Enlightenment philosophers occur allusions to Aesop and to the fables of Plato, Hesiod, and Ovid that are contained within their arguments, usually for the purposes of illustration and dramatization.

The pronouncements of various thinkers in the forms of maxims and adages often suggest narratives to develop in accord with their sentiments. Sometimes the analytic philosopher will adopt the poet's practice of personification of abstractions, and then a fable springs to life almost spontaneously. Here "Pru and Fancy" derives from Blaise Pascal's usage of that trope. Pascal (1623–1662) was a great mathematician and physicist as well as philosopher and devotional writer. It is not impossible that his figurative language colored his physics as well as his metaphysics.

Some of the problems Enlightenment philosophers set themselves concerned society, its origins and usages, its relationships to the state and the individual person, and to such social institutions as property and family. These are also subjects the Fables addressed. Ancient Fables dramatized those conflicts between the ideal and the actual that philosophers reasoned upon.

FOLKTALE

In general outline most fables are folktales. Fables are usually shorter in length; in fact, a fable might be described as a folktale reduced in size by continuous handling. Often it has gained point by means of wry humor. Yet it still bears those prominent characteristics of oral folk literature that make it attractive and easily portable.

To furnish the the first pages in Part IV I roughly whittled a few folktales into fable-form, using the traditional sources of folk and fairy tale collections like the brothers Grimm and including also the *Gesta Romanorum,* the compendium that inspired Boccaccio, Chaucer, Shakespeare and many other writers in later ages. I am hardly the first to give such materials fable presentation. La Fontaine's "The Man Who Buried His Treasure and His Crony" ("l'Enfouisseur et son Compère") is an exercise in this mode, a worthy model to try to emulate and a grateful acknowledgement by the French master of his homely sources.

In this part of the book, "The Story of Saint Felix" and "Birds and Priest" derive from the folktale form called the Saint's Legend. Other sources were selected at random to indicate the universality of the types.

PARABLE

A parable is shorter in length, but it is not an abbreviated fable. It tells a story and it may suggest a meaning, as do most fables. But it does not always reveal or demonstrate an obvious or even a clear message; in fact, several of the parables of Jesus are designed to present meanings open only to the initiated, as he tells us in the Gospel of Matthew, 13: 10–58.

The meaning of a fable may sometimes be puzzling, but the message of a parable can be purposely and suggestively mysterious. The message may be encoded upon the rationale given by the first-century poet Phaedrus:

> Now, here's the reason why I couch
> In fictive fables the matter I teach:
> The submissive slave will never dare
> To say his mind; he must forbear,
> Or transfer into fabulous form
> Truths that would cause him grievous harm.
> Book III, Prologue, 33–37

Phaedrus's fables may have been insufficiently mysterious; he was punished for their content by the ruthless consul Sejanus.

Parables well-suit nonviolent revolutionary agendas of thought and action; many of them could be described as counter-culture fables, especially those of Jesus, one-third of whose recorded words are contained in parables. For example, "The Wheat and the Tares" advises a revolutionary movement about what to do when membership has been infiltrated by informants.

These two latter readings are my own. Others will likely see the examples in a very different light. Compressing its substance into the smallest of packets, the parable invites and sometimes requires multiple explications.

Aesop. There are three different versions of the figure of Aesop. Herodotus (II, 134) identifies him as Thracian, the fellow slave of Rhodopis, the most famously beautiful courtesan of her time, in the sixth century BCE.

But Aristotle (*Rhetoric,* II, 20) tells us that he was a lawyer on the island of Samos who invented his fables as examples to illustrate his arguments and presentations. There is some possible vague overlapping of these two accounts.

The third Aesop is a legendary folk-figure slave to whom any popular fable or clever joke might be attributed as author, in the way that pointed apocryphal stories are said to originate with Abraham Lincoln, Will Rogers, W. C. Fields, Groucho Marx, and many another personality gifted with wit and wisdom. Evidence for this communal identification lies in the fact that at least twelve of the surviving classical fables include Aesop as a character.

Aesop is the humorous Anonymous. There can be no "definitive edition." Aesop is literature of and for the people and, assertively, by the people. Those who have borrowed his materials in later times have used them with utmost freedom, from Demetrius of Phalerum to Disney of Disneyland.

Avienus. Mid-fifth century Roman. I have included in this collection only one poem and part of another, having decided that David Slavitt's *The Fables of Avianus* (Johns Hopkins University Press, 1993) showcases the corpus in clear and entertaining fashion. My versions would be redundant and probably duller.

Babrius. Probably second century CE. Syrian by birth. One hundred forty-four fables, probably from a two-book collection, with plentiful borrowing from Aesopic tradition.

Phaedrus. Circa 15 BCE–CE 50. Thracian slave who became a freedman of Augustus. He claimed credit for raising the fable form to the stature of literature. His most frequently used source was of course, Aesop. Phaedrus made extensive use of *mythia,* the "morals" affixed to the stories.

The most sophisticated handler of the classical matter is *Jean de La Fontaine* (1621–95). A wary member of the artistic circle surrounding Louis XIV, he thoughtfully examined the customs and manners of his time through the lens of Aesop. Conversely, he examined Aesop from the perspective of the early Enlightenment, speculating upon the mechanics of animal and human behavior. The wit and polish with which he furnished his lines have been the despair of many an industrious translator. He did not treat his own sources with reverent devotion and later writers follow his example.

Metafable

Some fables are self-conscious; they reflect upon their own purposes and methods. Even some of those ascribed to Aesop bear this mark of sophistication, so that we may say of them, and of most fables, that they may be simple in construction and homely in manner, but they are not naive. They may adopt the pose of the *faux naif*, as Aesop often does; it is a strategy designed to expose the Know-It-Alls.

FOX

Fox is the most interesting of fable personae. Of the recorded tales more are concerned with Fox than with any other character.

He is a variable figure: skeptical, humorous, suspicious, diplomatic, dishonest, thieving, singular, and darkly clever. There are rumors that Fox invented the Old Shell Game, Three-Card Monte, and the Ponzi scheme.

And yet he is a good provider for his family, a trusted advisor to royalty and nobility, a compelling public speaker, a talented resolver of dilemmas and riddles, and an accomplished, though unlicensed, attorney-at-law.

His main strength is his keen knowledge of the nature of each of his fellow creatures. He finds their behaviors so predictable that he is usually two or three steps ahead of every one of them. At times he is too sharp for his own good and may maneuver himself into situations of utmost peril.

The Fabulist employs him as an investigative detective, an *agent provocateur,* a diplomat, a spy, and in other ambivalent, ambiguous roles. His social class too is ambiguous; he engages with ease among royalty and nobility as an accepted associate of Lions, Wolves, Apes, and Crows. He is on unfriendly terms with Shepherds, Farmers, and Hunters, but may sometimes join with them in some common cause. He engages with easy familiarity Horses, Asses, Bears, and Fabulists.

He is the prototype for such modern creations as O. Henry's Cisco Kid, E. W. Hornung's Raffles, Leslie Charteris's Saint, and many another gentlemanly crook. In a more sinister light, he is Iago.

Because he traipses at will across social boundaries, he is a useful observer for the narratives. The attitudes of his acquaintances toward him reveal facets of their own personalities.

Most sociable of beings, Fox is a loner at heart.